Future of Library and Information Science

Future of Library and Information Science

Festschrift Volume in
Honour of
DR. RAMAKANT SHARMA

Edited By
K. John
S. P. Singh
Sunil Tiwari

Ess Ess Publications
New Delhi

Future of Library and Information Science

ISBN: 978-81-7000-745-6

First Published 2015

Published by:
Ess Ess Publications
4831/24, Ansari Road,
Darya Ganj,
New Delhi-110 002.
INDIA
Phones: 23260807, 41563444
Fax: 41563334
E-mail: info@essessreference.com
www.essessreference.com

Cover Design by *Patch Creative Unit*

Printed and bound in India at Salasar Imaging Systems.

Contents

Dr. Ramakant Sharma

Dr. Ramakant Sharma is a well known name in the field of library and information science, not only in the Rewa but whole of Vindhya region. Dr. R. K. Sharma (Ramakant Sharma) was born on 03 August 1949 in a small village of Rewa District of Madhya Pradesh.

After completeing his Master's degree in chemistry, he was appointed teacher at Government Martand School No.3, Rewa. While working here, he completed B.Lib.Sc. from Govt. Thakur Ranmat Singh College, Rewa (Affiliated to Awadhesh Pratap Singh University, Rewa), M.L.I Sc. from Delhi University, Delhi and Ph.D. from Guru Ghasidas University, Bilaspur, Chhatisgarh.

He was appointed the Assistant Professor in the department of library & information science, Government Thakur Ranmat Singh College, Rewa (M.P.) on Jan. 1982 where he subsequently became the professor and head of department. During this period the department had started M.L.I.Sc and had become a Ph.D. and M.Phil. research centre.

Dr. R. K. Sharma had organized three national seminars sponsored by UGC in the years 1989, 1998 and

2012. Ten scholars got their Ph.D. under his able supervision. He has nine books on various aspects of library and information science to his credit and has more than twenty papers published in national and international research journals.

Dr. R. K. Sharma has also extended his services as Examination Controller in autonomous cell, Finance Controller and Chief Proctor in the College. He is also a visiting Professor in various universities in the India.

Dr. Sharma got *Motiwale Best Teacher* award in 2012.

Editors

Preface

The book entitled "Future of Library and Information Science" is not only a book but a treasure because it is the result of love, care, and cordiality shown by Dr. Ramakant Sharma during his long tenure as a teacher and mentor of students of library & information science. I am still amazed by the tremendous response of the scholars from all over India to this idea of bringing out a festschrift in his honour. It was an unambiguous culminating idea to release this book on the occasion of retirement of Dr. Ramakant Sharma.

Dr. N.R. Satyanarayana motivated us all throughout and extended his expertise to translate this idea into reality. The next hurdle during getting this book in its current shape was to decide a subject theme and the title of the book we thank Dr. N.R. Satyanarayana for his suggestion of not fixing the boundaries for the contributions because library and information science is a vast subject and it should not be restricted within boundaries. Therefore, we decided on a simple title for this book as *"Future of Library and Information Science"*.

As we are in the age of "Information", "Information Explosion" and "the Information Communication Technology" and this changing scenario has had a tremendous impact on our field. The book has become the information and the library with walls is now the library without walls, so how could we restrict the book into boundaries? Therefore the book without thematic barriers was proposed and has now become a reality on this auspicious occasion of superannuation of a personality like Dr. Ramakant Sharma.

It was also kept in mind that this book should commensurate the requirements of students, researchers and library professionals. It was a cumulative effort to materialize an idea; the authors have responded form all over the country. It took almost a year to complete this book but finally it sees the light of the day as our tribute to acknowledge the long services rendered by Dr. R.K. Sharma to our profession. I am very thankful to all contributors for contributing their valuable articles and suggestive inputs for this book.

I would like to end by quoting Charles Darwin ***"It is not the strongest of the species that survives, nor the most intelligent, but the one most responsive to change."*** I owe this to all contributors who have made this work possible with their invaluable responses. And last but not the least, I would like to record my appreciation for my co-editors Dr. S.P. Singh and Dr. Sunil Tiwari who extended their intellectual cooperation in whole process.

Editors

List of Contributors

Bajpai, Dr. R.P.
Associate Professor, LIS
MGCGV, Chitrakoot, Satna (MP)

Bajpai, Yogesh
Assistant Professor DLISc,
College of Natural and Computational Sciences
Mekelle University, Mekelle, Ethiopia

Begum, Shahbeena
Student, M. Phil.
Department of LIS Govt. T.R.S. College, Rewa (M.P.)

Chouksey, Dr. Shiv Sindhu

Gupt, Smt.Nidhi
Ass.Prof.Dr. C.V. Raman
Unversity kargi raod Kota Bilapspur)

Hada, Mr. Kapil Singh
JTA, Vansthali Vidya Pith, Rajsthan

Jha, Ajita
Student, M. Phil.
Department of LIS Govt. T.R.S. College, Rewa (M.P.)

John, Dr. Kishor
Asst. Professor, (OSD, Higher Education)
Moti Tabela Indore (M.P.)

Kumar, M. Kishore
Librarian
Jyothishmathi Institute of
Technological Sciences, Karimnagar

Kumar, Neeraj
Assistant Professor, D.S.College,
Gangtok (Sikkim)

Lalitha, R.
Librarian,
Jyothishmathi Institute of Technology Sciences

Mishra, Mr. Avinash
Librarian
Institute of Social Science, Indore (MP)

Naidu, Dr. GHS
Librarian
Central Library, Devi Ahilya University, Indore

Pandey, Ajay
Research Scholar, APS University, Rewa

Patel, Preeti
Research scholar

Prasad, Durga
Librarian, Central Digital Library
Shree Ganapti Institute of Technology Ghaziabad

Ratha, Bhupendra
Lecturer, School of LIS
Devi Ahilya University, Indore

Saini, Surbhi
UGC-NET, Research and Teaching Assistant
DLISc, School of Social Sciences, IGNOU, New Delhi

Sati, Dr. Prem Prakash
Dy. Librarian, Central Library
University of Petroleum & Energy Studies Dehradun

Sharma, Dr. Ashish Kumar
Assistant Librarian, Central library
Gurukul Kangri University, Haridwar

Sharma, Dr. Arvind K.
Asst. Professor, DLISc
M.L.B. Govt. College of Excellence, Gwalior

Sharma, Ku. Indubala
Librarian, Indore Institute of Law,
Opp. IIM, Indore

Shrivastava, Dr. Jitendra
Asst. Professor, DLISc
M. L. B. Govt. College of Excellence, Gwalior (M.P.)

Singh, Jyoti
Student, M. Phil.
Department of LIS Govt. T.R.S. College, Rewa (M.P.)

Soni, Sujeeta
Student, M. Phil.
Department of LIS Govt. T.R.S. College, Rewa (M.P.)

Sukhlal, Aske
M. Phil. in LIS Student
School of LIS, Devi Ahilya University,
Indore (M.P.)

Tamrakar, Dr. Rajnish
National Institute of Fashion Technology
M.P. Bhoj Open University Campus,
Kolar Road, Bhopal (M.P.)

Tiwari, Dr. Sunil Kumar
Guest Lecturer, LIS, Govt TRS College,
Rewa (M.P.)

Tiwari, Vijay Raghav
Scientific Officer (E)/Librarian
Harish-Chandra Research Institute
(Department of Atomic Energy,
Govt. of India), Allahabad (U.P.)

Tripathi, Deepika
Student, M. Phil.
Department of LIS Govt. T.R.S. College,
Rewa (M.P.)

Verma, Dr. Neerja
Professor & Head,
DLIS, M.L.B. Govt. College of Excellence,
Gwalior (M.P.)

Yadav, Dr. R.G.
Librarian, D.P. Vipra College Bilaspu

1
E-Literacy for Inclusive Development

Arvind K. Sharma
Assistant Professor
Department of Library and Information Science,
M.L.B. Govt. College of Excellence, Gwalior

ABSTRACT

This article deals with literacy, it defines the term literacy and e-literacy. Literacy is the multifaceted term which includes various types of activities. E- Literacy is a wide term. This term has gained more importance in the present electronic or digital environment. There are many synonyms terms used in the academia which as follows : ICT Literacy-1960's, Visual Literacy- 1969, Intelligent Tutoring Systems-1970's, Technological Literacy- 1970's, Information Literacy-1970's or 1980's, Computer Literacy- 1976, Academic Literacy, Digital Literacy, Multiliteracies, Media Literacy, Information commons – 1990's. The need of e-Literacy is discussed in detail. It can help in inclusive and sustainable development. Some figures are also provided to understand the phenomenon.

INTRODUCTION

The present era has two special features, i.e. competition and complexities. In present era competition has become a constant phenomenon, which cannot be ignored by any individual or group or any country. There is a complexity in our routine life. Today, one has to face competition and complexity simultaneously in the routine jobs and both are rising day by day. The question is how to deal with them? Literacy or e- literacy can help people in this regard. It is an instrument, which can answer our problems. Exploitation due to disinformation or misinformation can be minimized by literacy and inclusive development can be achieved.

Literacy is a complex term; it has different meanings in different contexts and society. It includes various types of activities and is an outcome of learning. Library and Information professionals should try to understand the depth of this term, especially academic and public library professionals, so accordingly, library services can be planned and executed.

LITERACY: MEANING

Literacy denotes the ability to read, write and understand. Literate person can easily participate in social, economic and academic activities of the community. Literacy is a basic human right of every citizen. It empowers a man to live with full dignity and respect. UNESCO says that literacy is :

- Ability to read and write[1].
- Ability of understanding.
- Participation in the academic activities.
- An outcome of learning.

This statement gives full understanding of term and includes multidimensional facets.

LITERACY : DEFINITIONS

There is no single definition to understand this term. Different definitions have different perceptions. UNESCO defines it as "The ability to identify, understand, interpret, create, communicate and compute, using printed and written materials associated with varying contexts. Literacy involves a continuum of learning enabling an individual to achieve his or her goals, develop his or her knowledge and potentials, and to participate fully in the community and wider society."[2] This definition is very vast and comprehensive and covers all aspects of literacy.

Harrod's Librarians' Glossary and Reference Book says (2005) "Literacy. The ability to read and write. More recently, the term 'literacies' is used to indicate a range of practical skills associated with information."[3] It is a simple definition associated with the information science.

ODLIS says that literacy is: The ability to read and write with a minimal level of proficiency.[4] It emphasizes on proficiency.

E-LITERACY : DEFINITIONS

E-Literacy is a wide term. This term has more importance in the present scenario of electronic or digital environment. Without it, one cannot find the path of progress and cannot cope up with the competition and complexities, which are increasing day by day in routine life of the people.

Harrod's Librarians' Glossary and Reference Book (2005) says -**E-literacy.** The skills required an individual to operate with maximum effectiveness in a global, electronic and information-rich environment.[5]

It is a skill, which is required by any individual to work efficiently and effectively in the present environment. Another definition, defines it other way: e-Lit (2003) – "A combination of information and computer literacy"[6] This definition combines the information and computer literacy. Librarians have great emphasis on literacies, so people can exploit maximum resources and take benefit of library services.

SYNONYMS TERMS

In the subject, other synonyms are also used to denote the same idea, these are enumerated below:

- ICT Literacy- 1960's
- Visual Literacy- 1969
- Intelligent Tutoring Systems- 1970's
- Technological Literacy- 1970's
- Information Literacy- 1970's or 1980's
- Computer Literacy- 1976
- Academic Literacy
- Digital Literacy
- Multiliteracies
- Media Literacy
- Information commons – 1990's

These all terms coined in different periods, and have the same objectives. They reflect a particular trend of development. These all terms coined in different places and have specific background.

E- LITERACY: WHY?

In the 21st century, people live in the world that is predominantly infused with the digital environment. More or less every part of the universe is affected by the term "e". Such as: e-banking, e-libraries, e-villages, e-health, e-books e-governance etc. In day to day life, people interact with e-world. ATM, ticketing, learning, communication etc. are the areas where people have to face challenges-literacy is needed to overcome this situation. Nowadays social media is being extensively used by the youngsters. Facebook, Twitter and WhatsApp are getting much importance. People can take advantages of these applications if they are e-literate. Others reasons are enumerated below:

For inclusive development: It is not so easy to take the benefits of schemes of Socio-economic development launched by the government. E-literacy is a media through which the public or common citizen can take the benefits of the various schemes. The gap of digital divide can be bridged by providing e-literacy to the people.

For strengthening the democracy: This term is very vast and incorporate various contexts and meanings.

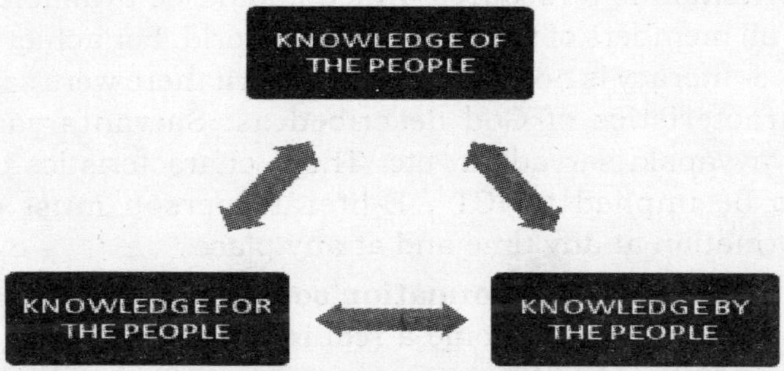

It is a trinity, all parts of this trinity are interrelated, interdependent or intertwined. They can't be separated from each other. If all members of the society are e-literate, naturally the democratic process will be more strengthened. An E-literate person can access, search, retrieve and evaluate the needed information and knowledge and use it in some context. E-literacy, democracy and development are interdependent terms in the present digital environment. E-iterate people can understand the depth of democratic values to great extent and they are also considerate towards others and have respect in democratization of resources. Ultimately development takes place in many ways.

or problem- solution environment : In the present world, there is a continuous, multifaceted and dynamic series of problems everywhere. E-literate person can search and find the solution of problems in a logical way.

For lifelong learning : Lifelong or throughout life

learning is a need of present society. E-literacy can help and boost the learning. Present societies have now become learning societies because without learning one cannot sustain and grow in this world. People have no choice or there is no alternate of lifelong learning. Taittiriyopnishad says " swadhyanmapramaditavyam" means 'never be lazy in learning.'

For universal availability of information : Information is a resource, which should be available to the all members of the society of the world. For achieving this e- literacy is needed. In the Sanskrit there were some characteristics of God described as: Sarvantaryami, sarvavyapak, sarvadhar, etc. These characteristics can also be implied to ICT . E-literate person must get information at any time and at any place.

For growing Information society : E-literacy can boost a society to become a real information society, in information society people are empowered with the weapon of e-literacy. With the weapon of e-literacy, people can fight against exploitation and protect their rights.

For quality education : Education is a lifelong process. In formal or informal education, people learn knowledge and skills to face the challenges in the right manner. E-literacy can add value to this process. In the Indian context it is very difficult to provide quality education to all the people living at distant places. E-literacy is medium, which can provide platform to facilitate equal and quality education among all citizens without discriminating poor or rich, near or distant etc.

For universal access to information : With the advent and diffusion of the ICT, it has become a reality that people can access information 24X7X365. Time and Distance have no meaning. Only e-literate people can get the benefit of ICT driven digital environment.

A table is given below, which shows the various phases of human civilization and its impact on various issues.

Items	Agrarian Society	Industrial Society	Information Society	Knowledge Society
Learning	One way process	Two way process	Interactive	More interactive
Economic resource	Material	Production	Information	Knowledge
Transfer of knowledge	Oral	Written	Multimedia	Interactive multimedia

For socio-economic development of society : Socio-economic development is the ultimate and supreme objective of any government or society. Each member of society should have equal opportunities to the resources. E-literacy can help in this regard.

IMPORTANCE OF E-LITERACY

Importance of e-literacy can be determined to great extent by its benefits. Societal and economic development can be achieved by diffusion of e-literacy. Freire, P. and Macedo.D. (1987) said "Literacy is a weapon against exploitation, and vehicle for emancipation and democracy."[7] In the present environment e-literacy is the only media, which can trigger or boost the socio-economic development of the people. For inclusive development e-literacy is a must.

A diagram is given below, which when seen clockwise expresses the cycle of learning and emphasizes on multiple literacy, because multiple literacy can solve the problems faced by the people.

For economic growth : For growth to happen economic development is needed. E-literacy can boost the economic development. Electronic transactions can save thousands of crores of rupees and protect environment by minimal use of paper. People must be e-literate for discouraging the physical money transactions.

For employability : E-literacy also generates lot of direct and indirect possibilities of employment. Knowledge

Process Outsourcing (KPOs), Business Process Outsourcing (BPO,s), Legal Process Outsourcing (LPOs), Call centres etc. provide job opportunities to youngsters.

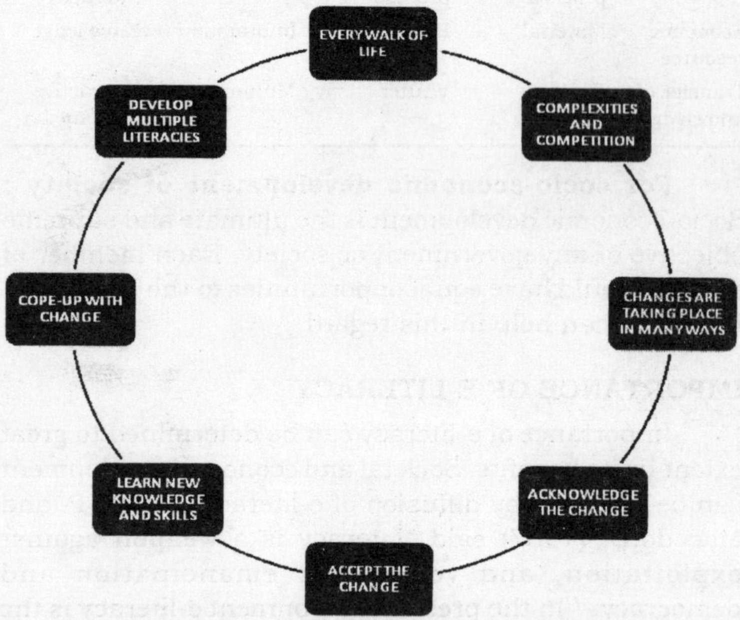

Fig. Cycle of learning

For cultured society : Literate or e-literate person can play a vital role in making cultured society. In cultured society human is the most precious wealth. E-literate person can help the members of the society objectively.

CONCLUSION

Literacy is a path on which civilizations have travelled and accessed the window of new world of harmony, brotherhood and cooperative way of life. Literacy especially e- literacy is the need of present society. A provision of free and universal access to information is needed for the development of every citizen. People cannot take the advantage of freely available information if they are not e- literate. In the present complex and ever-changing environment, multiple literacy is the key to solve the problems. Inclusive development can be achieved when we have consideration to strangers and have courtesy to others. Learning can help to a great extent to in this regard.

SUGGESTIONS

- E-literacy campaign should be organized for remote and distant people.
- Information literacy should be the part of Foundation courses at graduation level.
- People should be motivated to become an e-literate.
- One member of each family should be e-literate, for this purpose special schemes can be launched.
- Public libraries or Rural Information Centers should be promoted in urban and distant places of rural India.

REFERENCES

1. UNESCO. Literacy for life, Education for all: EFA Global Monitoring Report 2006. Paris : UNESCO, 2005.
2. The UNESCO program LAMP(Literary Assessment and Monitoring Programme) http://www.unesco.org/education/efa/global_co/working_group/WGEFA4_UIS. pt#268,15, Proposed definition)
3. Harrod's Librarians' Glossary and Reference Book ,Ray Prytherch(Comp.) Ashgate , Hampshire,2005.p.431.
4. http://www.abc-clio.com/ODLIS/odlis_l.aspx.
5. Ibid. p. 245.
6. e-Lit(2003) Second International Conference on Information and IT literacy, Glasgow Caledonian,Themes page,
7. Freire, P. and Macedo.D.(1987)Literacy: reading the world and the world, Westport, CT, Bergin & Garvey.

2

Future of Library and Information Science

Ajita Jha
MLISc, Department of Library & Information Science
T.R.S. College, Rewa(M.P.)
Deepika Tripathi
M.L.I. Sc., Department of Library in
T.R.S. Collage Rewa

1. INTRODUCTION

Whenever we think about library immediately it strike in our mind that we are talking about a place which gives knowledge, information, moral values etc. to millions of people around the world. We can not imagine any education system anywhere on globe without having library. The main objective of a library is not in collections of books but to provide a platform to its readers to enhance their knowledge. Any library have collection of newspapers (local, national, international), story books, novels, encyclopedia, journals, subject books etc. in regional or national languages. If we have to define library we can define it like this "A place where we can get information and knowledge on different topics, in the form of books is called as Library." Library is the most important place in any institute as students from different departments can get information on several topics from one single place. Almost all libraries have one librarian and one assistant librarian, one big hall, long tables and plenty of chairs for its readers. The role of librarian is very important in the management of library. Librarian is responsible for arranging books, newspapers and other study material in a proper and systematic way. He also maintains record of all above material in stock register. Nowadays as use of technology has increased in library all this work is also being done in computers. This new concept is called as "Digital Library". Librarian also makes sure the discipline, silence and maintenance of books and other material. Any library consists of open shelves and transparent close shelves. Expensive books are generally kept in closed shelves while routine books are kept in the open shelves.

2. HISTORY OF LIBRARY AND INFORMATION SCIENCE IN INDIA

India has very deep and old relationship with library system. According to facts and information library system was even found during the time period of Nalanda and Takshshila universities. The modern system of library science was introduced in India during 1930's. Some of the universities which started this system were university of Madras, AndhraUniversity, BHU, university of Delhi. When we talk about present situation almost all the universities are running various courses in Library and Information Science.

3. LEVELS OF EDUCATION IN LIBRARY AND INFORMATION SCIENCE

There has been a systematic, continuous and progressive change in Library and Information Science system and education in India. From informal to formal training, traditional library to digital library and certificate courses to diploma, degree and research courses have been implemented. Nowadays various universities are offering B.Lib., M.Lib., M.Phil., and Ph.D. programmes in Library and Information Science. Most of the universities are offering regular programmes while some universities are also offering distance education programmes. Some of the prestigious universities which are offering courses in distance education are Indira Gandhi National Open University (IGNOU), University of Madras, Annamalai University, Madurai-Kamraj University, B.R. Ambedkar University, H.S. Gaur university sagar and our own A.P.S. University Rewa. The main objective of distance education system is to provide opportunity to those professionals who are already in job and want to upgrade their qualification but don't have time for regular courses.

4. JOB OPPORTUNITIES IN THIS FIELD

Government is spending lot of money for school education as well as for higher education. Private sector has also contributed towards providing and developing quality education system. As a result of it numbers of aspirants are taking admission in school, colleges and universities. This has resulted in opening of number of private and government educational institution. After having a degree in Library and Information Science one can become librarian, assistant librarian, lecturer etc. in private and govt. institutions. Salary is also quite handsome as most of the institutes are paying as per 6'th pay commission. Salary starts from Rs. 10000 onwards and there is no upper limit. Librarian can also work as career counselor because most of the time they spend studying on different topics so they develop a deep sense of humor and good knowledge on various subjects.

5. ISSUES AND CHALLENGES

There are some issues and challenges in our system which should be taken seriously. One major problem is of lack of infrastructure in most of the government run and small institutions specially in rural areas. Another major issue is lack of training programmes, internship programmes and workshops for the students and professionals. We also need to update our syllabus and curriculum so that our students can compete with global demand. Most of the Library and Information Science institutions in India do not impart education on modern courses and hardly come up to the international standard. Most of the courses are theory-based. We need to add use of technology along with theory part.

6. USE OF TECHNOLOGY

We can not imagine a world without technology and similarly in the field of Library and Information Science technology can play very important and vital role. Effective use and implementation of technology will certainly make library system very interesting, easy to use, less paper work and smooth. We need to upgrade libraries by installing computers, I.C.T. etc. We can also use audio-visual C.D.'s for better learning. It is very important for us to convert our traditional libraries into digital and technology based libraries and these tools can certainly play an important role in this process. As it is an era of technology so use and effective implementation of E-Library can also be done. This will certainly help in the process of learning as by using E-Library one can search on different topics.

7. FUTURE OF LIBRARY AND INFORMATION EDUCATION IN INDIA

I believe that library science has not got its due respect and it is not being considered as a main career option by the students or their parents. In view of this, it is desirable that the library schools in India must adapt themselves to the changing situations so that they can turnout better professionals who can meet the challenges posed by the changing environment. Library schools that are not able to adapt themselves may become irrelevant and have to close down sooner or later in the years to come. But as a student of this field I see the positive side of it and I believe that it will cross all the hurdles and it will come in to main stream very soon.

8. CONCLUSION

Today, Library and Information Science education is no more an education for the mangers of libraries only, but has become an education for the consumers of knowledge also. We need to produce a new breed of professionals capable to successfully perform their role in the fast changing information needs of the society using new information technology and tools. We need to inculcate leadership quality, managerial skills, and techno savvy skills among our students and professionals. I have a very strong believe that future of library and information science is very bright and prosperous.

Finally I want to dedicate this paper to our respected Dr. R.K. Sharma Sir, who has served this institution for many years and successfully guided thousands of students through his knowledge and experience. I on behalf of all my seniors and juniors salute him for his dedication and commitment in shaping our life. I also request him to keep on guiding in future as well. Iwish him a very peaceful and long life.

REFERENCE

1. R. Todd et al., Summary of Reading the Future for Library and Information Services Education and Practice [Seminar], Education for Library and Information Services: Australia 14 (1997), 10–13.
2. B. Raymond, The future of library education in Australia – and its past, The Australian LibraryJournal 38 (1989), 115–123.
3. M. Buckland, Education for librarianship in the next century, Library Trends 34 (1986), 777–788.
4. P. Wilson, Bibliographical R & D, in: The study of information: interdisciplinary messages, F. Machlup and U. Mansfield, eds., New York, Wiley, 1983, pp. 389–397.

3

Role of Social Networks in Information Usage

R. Lalitha
Librarian, Jyothishmathi Institute of Technology Sciences
M. Kishore Kumar
Librarian, Jyothishmathi Institute of Technological Sciences Karimnagar,

ABSTRACT

In the library world, controlled vocabularies have long been created and maintained by professional catalogers for ease of retrieving relevant library materials. Recently, social tagging has been widely applied in many social network sites such as face book, twitter, Flickr etc. This phenomenon reflects the needs of online users for information organization and retrieval in online communities. Social network are increasingly attracting the attention of academic and industry researchers intrigued by their affordances and reach. This article deals with objectives of Social networks their usages and occurring problems while using social networks.

Key words : social networks, social tagging, online users.

INTRODUCTION

Social network is a new approach in libraries. These social network sites allow users to create pages in which others (professionally library users) can view and provide feedback. Some libraries have created an account in social network sites an attempt to promote and extend their library services. These social networking websites are becoming popular among students and professionals and help them in connecting with each other, their local and the global community at large.

After joining a social network site, users are prompted to identify others in the system with which they have a relationship. The label for these relationships differs depending on the site—popular terms include "Friends," "Contacts," and "Fans." Most SNSs require bi-directional confirmation for Friendship, but some do not. These one-directional ties are sometimes labeled as "Fans" or "Followers," but many sites call these Friends as well. The term "Friends" can be misleading, because the connection does not necessarily mean friendship in the everyday vernacular sense, and the reasons people connect are varied

The visibility of a profile varies by site and according to user discretion. By default, profiles on Friendster and Tribe.net are crawled by search engines, making them visible to anyone, regardless of whether or not the viewer has an account. Alternatively, LinkedIn controls what a viewer may see based on whether she or he has a paid account. Sites like MySpace allow users to choose whether they want their profile to be public or "Friends only." Face book takes a different approach—by default, users who are part of the same "network" can view each other's profiles, unless a profile owner has decided to deny permission to those in their network. Structural variations around visibility and access are one of the primary ways that SNSs differentiate themselves from each other.

AIMS AND OBJECTIVES

1. To find out the use of social networks by the professional users

2. To explore their views about the purpose of its use and trace the problems faced by them; and
3. To furnish the recommendations in this regard.

PURPOSE

Most of the users are frequently using these media for purchasing, video conferencing, selling, tagging related resources, advertisement, finding social contacts, ranking resources, earning money, finding communities of interest,. On the other hand sometimes they were using these media for making friends, sharing links, online learning, time passing, finding jobs online, news and for leisure/fun/entertainment .The rare use of these networks was for communication and research work.

Other social networks are noteworthy as well. Librarything enables users to catalog their books and view what other users share those books. The implications of this site on how librarians recommend reading to users are apparent. LibraryThing enables users, thousands of them potentially, to recommend books to one another simply by viewing one another's collections. It also enables them to communicate asynchronously, blog, and "tag" their books.

LIBRARY: SOCIAL NETWORKS

Libraries' role throughout history has been as a communal gathering place, one of shared identity, communication, and action. Social networking could enable librarians and patrons not only to interact, but to share and change resources dynamically in an electronic medium. Users can create accounts with the library network, see what other users have in common to their information needs, recommend resources to one another, and the network recommends resources to users, based on similar profiles, demographics, previously-accessed sources, and a host of data that users provide. And these networks would enable users to choose what is public and what is not, a notion that could help circumvent the privacy issues.

Library 2.0 .Of all the social aspects of Web 2.0, it could be that the social network and its successors most greatly mirror that of the traditional library. Social networks, in some sense, are Library 2.0. The face of the library's web-presence in the future may look very much like a social network interface.

BLOGS

The most obvious implication of blogs for libraries is that they are another form of publication and need to be treated as such. They lack editorial governance and the security this provides, but many are nonetheless integral productions in a body of knowledge, and the absence of them in a library collection could soon become unthinkable. This will, of course, greatly complicate collection development processes, and the librarian will need to exercise a great deal of expertise and fastidiousness when adding a blog to a collection

WIKIS

Wikis are essentially open web-pages, where anyone registered with the wiki can publish to it, amend it, and change it. Much as blogs, they are not of the same reliability as traditional resources, as the frequent discussions of wikipedia(an online encyclopedia where any registered user can write, amend or otherwise edit articles) in the library world well note; but this of course does not eliminate their value, it merely changes librarianship, complicates collection development and information literacy instruction. The lack of peer review and editorship is a challenge to librarians, not in that users should avoid wikis, but only in that they should understand and be critical in depending on them. Wikis as items in a collection, and the associated instruction of users in the evaluation of them, are almost certainly part of the future of libraries. Blogs and wikis are relatively quick solutions for moving library collections and services into Web 2.0.

TAGGING

Tagging essentially enables users to create subject headings for the object at hand. Tagging is essentially Web 2.0 because it allows users to add and change not only content (data), but content describing content (metadata). In Library 2.0, users could tag the library's collection and thereby participate in the cataloging process. The catalog of Library 2.0 would enable users to follow both standardized and user-tagged subjects; whichever makes most sense to them. In turn, they can add tags to resources. The user responds to the system, the system to the user. This tagged catalog is an open catalog, a customized, user-centered catalog. It is library science at its best.

RSS FEEDS

Rss feeds and other related technologies provide users a way to syndicate and republish content on the Web. Users republish content from other sites or blogs on their sites or blogs, aggregate content on other sites in a single place, and ostensibly distill the Web for their personal use. Libraries have yet to explore ways of using RSS more pervasively.

MASHUPS

Mashups are perhaps the single conceptual underpinning to all the technologies discussed in this article. They are ostensibly hybrid applications, where two or more technologies or services are conflated into a completely new, novel service.

Library 2.0 is a mashup. It is a hybrid of blogs, wikis, streaming media, content aggregators, instant messaging, and social networks. Library 2.0 remembers a user when they log in. It allows the user to edit OPAC data and metadata, saves the user's tags, IM conversations with librarians, wiki entries with other users (and catalogs all of these for others to use), and the user is able to make all or part of their profile public; users can see what other users have similar items checked-out, borrow and lend tags, and a giant user-driven catalog is created and mashed with the traditional catalog.

MYSPACE

The main features of the New MySpace are a "Type to Search" feature where the user simply starts typing and a search display screen appears with the most relevant hits for that search. Another feature is the streaming music player where users can queue songs, create mixes or playlists, or start a radio station .The overall layout of the New MySpace is a sideways scroll style where users scroll side to side rather than up and down.

While most libraries have switched from MySpace to Face book, the libraries listed have kept their MySpace pages active by connecting it to both their Twitter and Face book pages.

TWITTER

Twitter is an online social networking service and micro blogging service that enables its users to send and read text-based messages of up to 140 characters known as "tweets"

PIN REST

Pin rest is a pin board-style photo sharing website that allows users to create and manage theme-based image collections such as events, interests, hobbies, and more. Users can browse other pin boards for inspiration, 're-pin' images to their own pin boards, or 'like' photos.

CONCLUSION

The article presents a general trend of social media usage among the users of the library. It is encouraging that social media sites are using more for academic usage. The use of social media is rapidly increasing among young adults and students.The use of social media should be integrated with the conventional class room teaching and learning process; the teachers should enhance their skills in the use of these media, so they could be able to cope with these emerging global trends. Social media site operators should ensure online privacy and security. The multilingual features should be added on these sites, so more people representing different regions and languages can use these sites with great ease.

REFERENCE

- Boyd, D.M., & Ellison, N. B. (2007). Social network sites: definition, history, and scholarship. Journal of Computer-Mediated Communication, 13(1), article 11. Retrieved January 31, 2011, from http://jcmc.indiana.edu/vol13/issue1/boyd.ellison.html
- Cha, J. (2010). Factors affecting the frequency and amount of social networking site use: Motivations, perceptions, and privacy concerns. First Monday, 15, (12). Retrieved January 31, 2011, from http://www.uic.edu/htbin/cgiwrap/bin/ojs/index.php/fm/article/viewArticle/2889/2685
- Maness, J.M. (2006). Library 2.0 theory: Web 2.0 and its implications for libraries. Webology, 3(2), article 25. Retrieved November 29, 2010, from http://www.webology.org/2006/v3n2/a25.html
- O'Reilly, T. (2005). Web 2.0: compact definition. Retrieved November 29, 2010, from http://radar.oreilly.com/archives/2005/10/web-20-compact-definition.html
- Acquisti, A., & Gross, R. (2006). Imagined communities: Awareness, information sharing, and privacy on the Facebook. In P. Golle & G. Danezis (Eds.), *Proceedings of 6th Workshop on Privacy Enhancing Technologies* (pp. 36-58). Cambridge, UK: Robinson College.
- Adamic, L. A., Büyükkökten, O., & Adar, E. (2003). A social

network caught in the Web. *First Monday, 8* (6). Retrieved July 30, 2007 from http://www.firstmonday.org/issues/issue8_6/adamic/index.html

- Backstrom, L., Huttenlocher, D., Kleinberg, J., & Lan, X. (2006). Group formation in large social networks: Membership, growth, and evolution. *Proceedings of 12th International Conference on Knowledge Discovery in Data Mining* (pp. 44-54). New York: ACM Press.

4

Changing Role of Public Libraries in 21st Century and LIS Education

R. P. Bajpai
Associate Professor LIS, MGCGV, Chitrakoot, Satna (MP)
Kapil Singh Hada
JTA, Vansthali Vidya Pith, Rajsthan
Avinash Mishra
Librarian, Institute of Social Science, Indore(MP)

ABSTRACT

Public library has power to communicate, to disseminate knowledge and information among community of society and also plays an important role in provide information to relating social-economic, political and education. This paper is discussed about the role and important of public libraries in development of any community through their services.

Key Words : Public Library, Rural Community, ICT's, UNESCO.

INTRODUCTION

Information explosion and the fast development of information technology forced libraries to adopt the faster methods of information storage and retrieval devices. Public libraries are no exception to this change. The public libraries have to adopt this change to meet the ever changing needs for the collection building organization and retrieval of information are the basic functions of library and also provide pinpointed and faster service and information to their clientele. The manual methods are unable to show solutions to the ever growing information. Keeping in view of the information explosion, advancement of ICT's and development of information seeking society uses of ICT's in libraries the only solution for storage and retrieval of information.

The Public Libraries, as the extended versions of Knowledge Centre have to undertake the work of collecting, organiszing, disseminating both knowledge and information, in coordination with other institutions and experts, using ICT's and guidance of the management and subject experts, collection information/knowledge under and interrelated system so that duplication is avoided, knowledge is pooled systematically, it is used, and also forwarded to national knowledge centre, for wider use in various experts. It also takes into account knowledge available locally and makes it available in local languages.

(IGNOU 2003) : Public library has been emerged as an important social institution. "This social Institution set up and working is based on the definition of democracy. It is for the people, by the people and of the people.

According to Ronald Benge, the concept of public library consists of four elements;

- The public libraries are available for loan of materials and for reference purposes to all citizens;
- The public libraries are mainly supported from public funds either on a local or a national basis;
- The services should be free to all individuals;
- The material should be made available as an integral part of right.

Prof Viswanathan (1965), "Public libraries are run by the people, for the people as a public organization. The foundation and conservation of public libraries should be done under clear authority of law. They should be managed by the public fund basically and be available for the whole social community without any discrimination such as class, creed, sex etc, in a democratic way.

The UNESCO Public Library Manifesto (1994) declares that constructive participation and the development of democracy depends on satisfactory education to as well as on free and unlimited access to knowledge, thought and information. Ensuring access to citizens to all sorts of community information services and facilitating the development to information and computer literacy skills have been included in the missions of the Manifesto. The public library is a social institution. The purpose of which is "to educate" to inform" and "to entertain" the public. Its importance is more than that of formal institution for education, such as schools, colleges and universities.

According to the Advisory Committee for Libraries (1959), the internationally accepted definition of public library is that, it is a library which;

- Is financed for the most part from the public funds;
- Charges no fees from the readers and yet it is open for full use to the public without distinction of class, creed or sex;
- Is intended as an auxiliary educational institution providing a means of self education which is endless and
- Houses learning materials giving reliable information freely without partiality or prejudice on a wide variety of subjects as well satisfy the interest of readers.

PUBLIC LIBRARY AS COMMUNITY INFORMATION CENTRE

Public library as an institution not so much for the storage, preservation and dissemination of knowledge and public library is a public institution being run for the people, of the people and by the people. The library is also analogous to a temple whose internal atmosphere is in no way less than a religious place to be it is like a temple. A public library is one which is open to full public use. It is the property of the general public. The development of ICT's has left no area of society and also further advancement of communication technology, storage media, World Wide Web (WWW) and internet is also affecting and change the role of public libraries. Hence the buzz "Public Libraries as a Knowledge Centres", Public Libraries as an Information Kiosks", and Public Libraries as a Community information Centres". So in 21st century public libraries have been making a great impact in the area of education, recreation, cultural activities, social welfare, social and political development.

For transforming the rural libraries into active community information centres the infrastructure of these libraries has to be improved. They may be provided one set of computer, printer, scanner, UPS, fax and photocopying machines and internet link. The improved facilities will also enable them to serve as literacy centres in rural areas. This will not only help in improving the literacy rate, but also sustaining the literacy of the neo-literates and thereby promoted the objectives of the National Literacy Mission.

Community Information Centres can play a vital role in the rural areas for development of rural community to:

- Find information on subjects of interest to them and to take part in learning activities;
- To collect and disseminate knowledge and

information among the different rural communities;

- Enjoy cultural and leisure activities;
- Use equipment to produce their own information materials;
- Meet to organize and work together on community projects

PUBLIC LIBRARIES AND WOMEN EMPOWERMENT

Today women play a vital role in all the area of development, so we can not the women power in the twenty first century. But in Indian conditions is very different from the others country, especially in rural area. There are about the 50 % of women are illiterate, so public libraries are play an important role in it. Awareness of women empowerment may be promoted through the public libraries via community information center in especially rural area.

PUBLIC LIBRARIES AND RURAL DEVELOPMENT

The role of public libraries in the rural areas can be multi-dimensional and may have cascading effect on the overall development scenario. They can act as effective intermediaries. They can provide direct linkage missing so far between the various agencies meant to take care of villages. Village's library can act as a hub for all the activities of a village whether it is meeting of the Panchayat or the organization of exhibition/show, cultural activities discussions and as dissemination of information related to any new government initiatives or schemes. The primary goal of rural library should be dissemination of information, keeping alive the cultural heritage enhancing vocational competence and encourage learning, reading and writing amongst the general masses. It is through the public library that information could be dissemination to all, irrespective of age.

PUBLIC LIBRARIES AND CONTINUING EDUCATION

Education plays an important role in the overall development of an individual; public library should be the living force behind it. It should cover all sections of the society including the illiterate, neo-literate, semiskilled, children and youth. If the public library system reaches the grass roots levels that is villages, the rural library will take care of neo-literate and provide them relevant materials. It should create reading habits among the rural people through distribution of books, display of attractive pictures and news papers. These materials should be related to better techniques of farming, new seed technology, pesticides, good health, family planning programmes, cultural values, small savings others activities related to social evils, which fulfilled the purpose of rural libraries .(Khosla, 2003).

The public libraries are now considered as the people's university. Its functions are not educational but informal. The philosophy and objective behind continue education is informal rather than academic. One of the significant functions of the public library is to provide platform for discussion groups and forums.

PUBLIC LIBRARIES AND SOCIAL DEVELOPMENT

Public library has an important role to play in national programme of social reconstruction and nation building. A librarian in the rural areas should not be a custodian of books but also a provider of authentic information to their users. Public library can develop the character and conduct of the rural people and gives knowledge regarding social sciences. It can also help care social problems like child marriage, evils of dowry system, superstitions belief, drug addiction, communalism and regionalism and crime against women and so on.

PUBLIC LIBRARIES AND KISOSKS

The 21st century the role changing for the public

libraries. The public libraries are playing an important role in the education, life learning and continuing education these libraries provided their users all the concern materials. In this era all the information are available in the digital form and also information to be digitized and these information accessible through networks. It is the challenging jobs for the public libraries and their professional, not only to provide information on the networked and also provide the information their users in the different form. Public libraries should be able to give the information to right users in right form at the right time with the help of modern technology and equipment. A Knowledge Information Centres or KIOSKS, it should be established in public libraries and managed by public libraries authorities. In these section also provided information in the form books, news papers, journals, gray literature, educational CD's, audio cassettes, internet facilities at cheapest rates, education based databases, latest information related government policies, announcement.

PUBLIC LIBRARIES AND E-LEARNING

Teaching is an act of creating a learning situation to impart knowledge, stimulate the thought processes and encourage individual development. *"Education is not filling a bucket but kindling a lamp"*. Public libraries will play an important role in development and progress of any community for any particular area, society, place or a country. It provides any information to their communities for fulfill particular information. Public library is related to direct to the public. The public library will play a vital role in e-learning area. E-learning is the change all the traditional way of teaching methods, it is offering virtual classrooms to a without geographical boundaries and countries, it is revolutionizing change in the educational system; it is also focusing on individual rather than a group. We can say that it is totally personally attention teaching methods. E-learning is transfer to the knowledge from one to many people or groups. It also reduces cost, infrastructure, salary of faculty members and administrative members and also increasing satisfaction of student. The satisfaction of student is must for each and every educational system. The major change in e-learning with satellite and television expansion and also advancement in the field of telecommunication is also affect the e-learning process. The Television can also change the education system. On the television, we can broadcast the educational based program, where the people can learn from it and also benefit. People can learn anything, at low cost, at anytime, anywhere, any subject on their television set at home. Public libraries are considered as an essential part of a modern society, and play a very important role to support information for rural development. An effective public library system is a prime need of social, political, cultural, economic, scientific and technological fulfillment for any democratic set up. (Devi, Tanuja and Devi, Madhuri, 2004).

PUBLIC LIBRARY AND LITERACY PROGRAMME

The Adult Education Programmes such as Sarve Shiksha Mission and other educational programme started for the village rural communities by the State Government may be amalgamated with village library function. The libraries have plays an important role in eradication of illiteracy. Government of India initiated 'community Development Programme', in which social education was assigned an important role.

The libraries become an integral part of this programme. *In document on National Policy on Library and Information System*, it has recommended Public Library services be also supported by the agencies involved in social education, rural interest for books among villages so as to generate the habit of reading in a slow but deliberated process. The School library should be kept open during the vacation and long holidays for the benefit of students as well as the local community.

PUBLIC LIBRARY AND SCHOOL LIBRARY

The formal education institutions are not the only means of imparting education in the rural areas. Education is also impacted by other others informal and non formal educational centres such Shiksha Kendra, Anaphoric Shiksha Kendras, Aganwadi Kendra. The School libraries and village libraries should play their useful role in the activities of these centres.

The Advisory Committee for Libraries (1958) also recommended that school libraries be serves as public libraries after school hours and to implement the recommendation. The school library as public libraries is benefits of newly literates, farmers and artisans. The school library also have key role in village life. *In document on National Policy on Library and Information System,* it has recommended Public Library services be also supported by the agencies involved in social education, rural interest for books among villages so as to generate the habit of reading in a slow but deliberated process. The School library should be kept open during the vacation and long holidays for the benefit of students as well as the local community.

The National policy on Education 1986, recommended that 'together with development of books, a nation-wide movement for improvement of existing libraries and the establishment of the new ones will be taken up and provision will be made in all educational institutions for improved library facilities".

PUBLIC LIBRARIES AND DISTANCE EDUCATION

The distance education programme should be supported by the Public Libraries. The study centre of IGNOU, M. P. Bhoj (Open) Vishwavidyalaya and open

School should be opened in the public libraries where available.

PUBLIC LIBRARY AND VILLAGE KNOWLEDGE CENTRE

Today we are living in the era of Information and Communication Technology and India is also Software giant. About the 65 % of Indian community lives in rural areas, but there is no such facility to access the latest information. The Rural Public Libraries are in existence at village level. The Rural Public Library yet to adopt the ICT in their routine works and no proper ICT infrastructure for libraries. The Rural Public Libraries face stiff challenges in providing basic library facilities to their clienteles. The Rural Public Libraries lack in fund and facilities. But at the same time the library professionals/staff working in these libraries is very much committed. The time has come to establish, expand Public Rural Libraries, services even to the remote area for the development of the rural masses at grass root level. Rural Public Libraries gave an opportunity to rural community who want overall development of the rural masses in the area of economic, education, culture. These libraries can play a very positive role which can be regarded as the nerve centre of the rural area development. The Rural Public Library services are considered an important part of it. Village Knowledge Centre is one step towards fulfill these gap. Village Knowledge Centre is gave new dimension to the libraries and libraries professionals. Village Knowledge Centre gave an opportunity to Rural Public Libraries to improving ICT infrastructure. It should be established in each and every Rural Public Library. With the help of village knowledge centre the Rural Public Libraries serve in better ways to their community and clientele. It will be provide a new avenue to the modernization of public library specially Rural Public

Library. The combination of Village Knowledge Centre and gave an opportunities to rural community to participate in e-governance effectively and also provide library services to maximum satisfaction to the rural community. It will be ease the digital divide in between urban and rural community. If Village Knowledge Centre is established in each and every Rural Public Library, libraries get the revenue from their services, and it will be ease the dependency on the government for the finance purpose. The Village Knowledge Centre will also provide trained manpower and as well as ICT infrastructure to the Rural Public Library. It will be beneficial for the Library.

PUBLIC LIBRARIES AND USERS WITH SPECIAL NEEDS

Public libraries provide access to services to people with disabilities. This can be easier said than done in some libraries within old buildings that are difficult to make accessible. Physical improvement is the most viable way of ensuing disabled users can gain access, including installing ramps for wheelers and perhaps and elevators for libraries that have multiple floors.

PUBLIC LIBRARIES AND MINORITIES

Public libraries have offered pathways into the social life and culture. Public libraries offer a ideal venue for members of minorities to know that society values their culture through access to works in their mother tongue, or related to their religion or culture. As people who live in the community and pay taxes they have legal and moral right to expect library services be provided for them. The public libraries build a collection that represents the culture of the community and also translated for users who do not speak local language.

PUBLIC LIBRARIES AND REFUGEES AND ASYLUM SEEKERS

Public libraries should serve with immigrants and refugee communities. As part of its remit is developed a good practice guide aimed at informing public library staff about the issues inherent in dealing with refugee and asylum seeker communities, and the policies they needed to be aware of in providing services. It also offered advice and contact details for further information on service development for this community (Vincent, 2007).

PUBLIC LIBRARIES AND HOUSEBOUND SERVICES

Housebound services are a crucial tool in facilitating social inclusion of library services. These services are offered those persons, who are unable to come to the library. The common model is for users to register with the library service and to receive a regular (normally monthly) visit from a volunteer or library staff member who will bring books. Titles are selected according to the response a user gives on a questionnaire asking about their tastes. Library staff then put together a range of titles for them based on their stated preferences.

CONCLUSION

The role of public libraries is drastically changed in present time due to information explosion and invention of information communication technology. The Importants of public libraries is not recognized as they have. The public libraries play an important role to discuss above point. Public library gave not important in Indian scenario of library and information education they have. I urged to teacher community of LIS education trying to include public library as a paper in current syllabus. If is possible in future, we hope that changing mind set about people for public libraries.

REFERENCES

- Vyas, S. D., Public Library System (Jaipur: Deepmala Prakashan, Jaipur, 1992), 11-13.
- Vishwanathan, C.G., Introduction to Public Library Organization (Mumbai: Asian Publishing House, 1965), 1.
- Augustine, C.A. and Deverajan, G, Public Library System in India,(New Delhi, Ess Eṣs: New Delhi, 1990), 33-34.
- Beguam,D and Goswami A., "Development of Public Libraries and Library Legislation in Assam," Herald of Library Science 42 (2003): 170-177.
- Jatana, M and Khosla, S., "Public Library: A dynamic community centre for social-cultural uplift of Rural India," Herald of Library Science 42 (2003): 66-73.
- Adinanayana Reddy, "Facts of Continuing Education", University News 28(1990):6-12.
- UNESCO Library Manifesto, 1994.
- IGNOU, "Public Library System and Services", IGNOU (2003):3

5
Cloud Computing

Vijay Raghav Tiwari
Scientific Officer (E) / Librarian
Harish-Chandra Research Institute
(Department of Atomic Energy, Govt. of India)
Allahabad (U.P.)

MEANING : WHAT IS CLOUD COMPUTING?

"Cloud computing" is not a precise term, with various definitions given; some examples: According to Wikipedia: "Cloud computing is Internet-based computing, whereby shared resources, software, and information are provided to computers and other devices on demand, like the electricity grid." (*http://en.wikipedia.org/wiki/Cloud_computing*) VMware, a company involved in providing software and services, offers a more business-oriented definition: "Cloud computing is a new approach that reduces IT complexity by leveraging the efficient pooling of on-demand, self-managed virtual infrastructure, consumed as a service." (*http://www.vmware.com/ap/cloud-computing.html*).

The main idea of cloud computing is to build a virtualized computing resource pool by centralizing abundant computing resources connected with network and present the service of infrastructure, platform and software. This network that offers various computing resources is called "cloud" . As a supercomputing paradigm based on the Internet, cloud computing allows customers to dynamically share a mass of hardware, software and data resource, and charges according to their actual usage.

The term "cloud computing" is used quite freely, tagged to almost any type of virtualized computing environment or any arrangement where the library relies on a remote hosting environment for a major automation component. It's as much a marketing term as a technical one. Some of its characteristics include:

- An abstract technology platform that involves generalized access to remote computing resources rather than locally owned and managed discrete servers
- A utility model of computing involving fees charged for levels of use rather than capital investments in hardware or permanent software licenses Computing that's provisioned on demand, with resources allocated as needed
- Elastic quantity and power of the computing resources that increase at times of peak use and scale down when demand is lower
- Highly clustered and distributed computing infrastructure that spreads computing tasks across many devices to maximize performance with high fault tolerance for the failure of individual components

If you've used any of the popular Web 2.0 services over the past few years (e.g. Gmail, Wikipedia, Flickr or Twitter), you already have some experience with cloud computing, since most of these applications are hosted in the large online data centres that are the hallmark of cloud computing.

BASIC NEED FOR CLOUD COMPUTING

- On-demand self-service
- Broad network access
- Resource pooling
- Location independence
- Rapid elasticity
- Measured service

HOW TO EXPLORE

Cloud computing is proposed by Google firstly. According to the definition of cloud computing given by the U.S. National Institute of Standards and Technology (NIST) and other authoritative agencies, cloud computing can be explained through the virtualization and other technology, a large number of server clusters connected by networking are logically integrated as one super cloud server with mass storage and supercomputing capabilities. So that this super cloud server can provide secure, convenient data storage and fast computing services to users through the network according to certain public rules. In the cloud computing mode, the user's data and computing do not run in the their terminal equipment such as personal computers, but in the cloud server through network. So that, user can access to more resources (such as data and computing, etc.) through sharing others resources.

USES/BENEFITS

Databases are the preferred way of persisting structured data powering web applications. Cloud service providers have tuned and rewritten database functionality for the cloud, opening up new opportunities for scalable data services across multiple dynamic application instances. Cloud databases are distributed, replicated, and largely transactional. Cloud databases can be separated from the rest of the cloud stack through

Restful APIs between different vendors but there is a definite latency advantage to coupling of data and its interpreter.

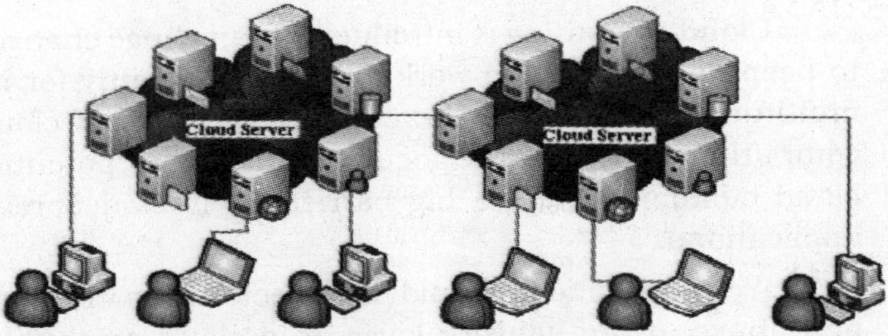

It contains the following benefits too:

Data Fragmentation and Dispersal : Since the data is place at different places and managed by highly experienced professionals, it contains all possible care for its retrieval.

Dedicated Security Team : Because of the huge quantity of the data from different sources, a very highly qualified and experienced team works seamlessly on the security aspects too which is much more advanced that the normal nodes/

Greater Investment in Security Infrastructure : Considering the security aspects of the data and reliability, huge investment in security is provided.

Fault Tolerance and Reliability : It contains almost zero degree tolerance in reliability field to provide maximum safe data storage and retrieval.

Greater Resiliency : Data access is quite smooth and reliable because of the highly sophisticated management of the data storage.

Hypervisor Protection Against Network Attacks: Presently popular hacking attempts on the server is also taken care of, due to the highly dedicated professional coverage of the data.

Possible Reduction of C&A Activities (Access to Pre-Accredited Clouds)

DATA SECURITY ASPECTS

Cloud computing is introducing many huge changes to people's lifestyle and working pattern recently for its multitudinous benefits. However, the security of cloud computing is always the focus of numerous potential cloud customers, and a big barrier for its widespread applications.

Web applications should be protected from intrusion and abuse at the network layer. In a cloud computing world application security is a lot like click fraud in advertising: every bad action carries a marginal cost. Cloud providers need to guard customers against potential external abuse and intrusion.Google, Microsoft, and Amazon have their eyes on many incoming requests each day. Google serves App Engine requests off the same hardware handling Google Front End, keeping bad requests away from search, ads, and your apps.The effect of the growing dependence on cloud computing is as necessary as it is necessary to use public transportation instead of using your own vehicle which cost a lot and gives more pollution too . On the other hand, if we consider it economically it will be more feasible too because of being cost effective it will be used in more occurrences. The physical safety can be much more higher as storage would be a specific concern of the Data Storage Center.

IT HAS SOME PROBLEMS OF BREACH

The analogy is interesting, but air travel is fairly safe. So how serious are today's cloud computing security problems, really?

It depends on your viewpoint. From the view of a broad class of potential users it is very much like trusting the telephone company–or Gmail, or even the post office–to keep your communications private. People frequently place confidential information into the hands of common carriers and other commercial enterprises.

There is another class of user who would not use the telephone without taking security precautions beyond trusting the common carrier. If you want to procure storage from the cloud you can do the same thing: never send anything but encrypted data to cloud storage. On the other hand, if you want the cloud to do some actual computing for you, you don't have that alternative.

What about all of the interesting new research pointing the way to encrypted search and even encrypted computation in the cloud?

The whole point of cloud computing is economy: if someone else can compute it cheaper than you can, it's more cost effective for you to outsource the computation. It has been shown to be possible in principle for the computation to be done on encrypted data, which would prevent the person doing the computing from using your information to benefit anyone but you. Current techniques would more than undo the economy gained by the outsourcing and show little sign of becoming practical. You can of course encrypt the data between your facility and the elements of the cloud you are using. That will protect you from anyone other than the person doing the computing for you. You will have to choose accountants, for example, whom you trust.

SECURITY FEATURES

1. Traditional Security Practice Mechanism

Traditional security practice such as the security protection of physical facilities, network, computer system, software application, and data still work in a cloud environment, and constructing a cloud environment should obey the common international information security standards such as ISO27001. Therefore, the traditional security practice mechanisms should be assured for a secure cloud environment.

2. Virtualization Security Risks Assessment

Regardless of a public or private cloud, the construction and deployment of a cloud environment cannot lack numerous virtualization products. Therefore, we need to assess the merits and drawbacks and security level of various virtualization technology resolutions and suite products, and choose the best one to reduce the security risks brought by virtualization.

3. Development Outsourcing Risk Control

Constructing a cloud environment is a large-scale systematic engineering with heavy work load and many advanced technologies, so it is hard to take charge of all development work for an organization. A practical action is to handover partial development work to several outsourcing parties, which will introduce some security risks. Therefore, we should identify the security risks incurred by outsourcing service and establish strict control strategies to assure their quality level and security requirement.

4. Portability and Interoperability

Customers must keep in mind that they may have to change service providers for the sake of unacceptable cost increase at contract renewal time, business operations ceasing by service providers, partial cloud service closure without migration plans, unacceptable service quality decrease, and business dispute between cloud customer and provider etc. Therefore, portability and interoperability should be considered up front as part of the risk management and security assurance of any cloud program.

Security options available with us :

- Trusting vendor's security model
- Customer inability to respond to audit findings

- Obtaining support for investigations
- Indirect administrator accountability
- Proprietary implementations can't be examined
- Loss of physical control

1. Use in Libraries

Libraries may soon be building and managing their own data centers. In addition to all the hype and optimism surrounding cloud computing, there are still significant fears and doubts *Industry Challenges* points out. In particular, the major cloud computing vendors haven't yet fully addressed concerns about security, privacy and reliability. These concerns are leading some companies to build their own private or hybrid clouds. A hybrid cloud is primarily based in a privately-owned and operated data center, but it can shift some of its traffic and data processing requests to public cloud vendors such as Amazon or Rackspace on an as needed basis. This hybrid model would let libraries maintain more control over the applications and data stores that contain sensitive, private information about patrons. Moreover, libraries can continually adjust and fine-tune the balance between the tight control of a private IT infrastructure, and the flexibility and savings of cloud-hosted infrastructure. If reliability or security of one vendor becomes a concern, you're not committed to one company or one model of computing services. Moreover, if the thought of "building and managing your own data center" sends chills down your spine, you might consider a community cloud. Google plans to launch a government-only cloud this year to address government concerns about security and privacy. Just as libraries presently cooperate with one another to buy IT equipment, bandwidth and the services of IT professionals, libraries may soon cooperate in the building and management of data centers. Alternately, if enough libraries express interest, a company such as Google, Amazon, Microsoft or another cloud vendor might create a Library Cloud similar to Google's Government Cloud. Or, a library vendor with deep IT resources (e.g. OCLC or SirsiDynix) might build library-centric cloud services on top of cloud infrastructure leased from one of the more established players.

Examples : Cloud computing–programs and services delivered over theInternet–is rapidly changing the way we use computers. Gmail, Twitter, and Facebook are all cloud applications, for example. Web-based infrastructure services like Amazon's–as well as versions from vendors such as Rackspace–have attracted legions of corporate and institutional customers drawn by their efficiency and low cost. The clientele for Amazon's cloud services now includes *the New York Times* and Pfizer. And Google's browser and forthcoming operating system (both named Chrome) mean to provide easy access to cloud applications.

To date, the main focus of libraries moving into the cloud has been discovery services, the need to disclose their vast collections on the Web. Though library OPACs attract existing patrons they are not integrated with most information seekers common workflows. So a first step for libraries has been to start massively aggregating data about their collections into common pools. OCLC's WorldCat, the first example of this, is now forty years old and pre-dates both the Web and cloud computing. Other similar union catalogs have existed throughout the world most commonly supported by national libraries and large union catalogs, such as the National Library of Australia, the Bayerische Staatsbibliothek in Germany, and Bibsys in Norway. However the advent of the Web has allowed libraries to extend this original vision in new ways. Extending these services beyond traditional library collections is well illustrated by the National Library of Australia's (NLA) Trove. It has used the Web to accomplish two tasks. This is done by first combining the collections of Australian libraries with other important Australian and international collections and information sources such a Wikipedia and secondly to open much of this content so the public can tag it, edit it, collect it and review it. The explosion of digitization projects in the last decade has driven this gathering of information in new directions with examples in addition to NLA's Trove to others like the Hathi Trust, OAISTER and Europeana. The Hathi trust is building a repository of digitized books and journals from major research libraries in the United States. OAISTER is a service started by the University of Michigan and now managed by OCLC which seeks to harvest all the major digital repositories around the world. Europeana is gathering the digitized collections from Europe's galleries, libraries, archives and museums. What makes these aggregations and others like them important is their intent to allow their content to be mashed up into other services and re-used. Other benefits growing from massively aggregated data about collections is the ability to aggregate user opinion and use. LibraryThing is a good example of being able to build recommender services based on the aggregation of what thousands of people hold in their personal libraries. However, there is no reason to extend cloud-based services only to libraries' end users. As Marshall Breeding points out, "We can't let the current focus on front-end interfaces make us complacent about the software systems that we use to automate routine library functions."

CONCLUSION

Cloud computing is a kind of computing paradigm that can access conveniently a dynamic and configurable public set of computing resources (e.g. server, storage, network, application and related service), provided and published rapidly and on-demand with least management and intervention. However, the prevalence of cloud computing is blocked by its security to a great extent.

Libraries have the opportunity to improve their services and relevance in today's information society. Cloud computing is one avenue for this move into the future. It can bring several benefits for libraries and give them a different future. The cooperative effect of libraries using the same, shared hardware, services and data—rather than hosting hardware and software on behalf of individual libraries—can result in lowering the total costs of managing library collections and enhancing the both library user's experience and library staff workflows. While local library systems served an important purpose earlier in library automation they now represent a tremendous duplication of effort. Each library builds and maintains a database, buys equipment and installs and updates the software. In fact, some libraries can get stuck in perpetual upgrade mode, which involves lots of testing and retesting and time-consuming customization.

With cloud computing, all of this is taken care of transparently for the library and user.

Among the benefits of a cloud computing approach:

- Take advantage of current and rapidly emerging technology to fully participate in the Web's information landscape
- Increased visibility and accessibility of collections
- Reduced duplication of effort from networked technical services and collection management
- Streamlined workflows, optimized to fully benefit from network participation
- Cooperative intelligence and improved service levels enabled by the large-scale aggregation of usage data
- Make libraries greener by sharing computing power thus reducing carbon footprints

The vision is to use cloud computing to deliver library resources, services and expertise at the point of need, within user workflows and in a manner that users want and understand. It should free libraries from managing technology so they can focus on collection building, improved services and innovation. The cloud computing model will encourage libraries and their users to participate in a network and community of libraries by enabling them to reuse information and socialize around information. It can also create a powerful, unified presence for libraries on the Web and give users a local, group and global reach.

Community library is very important, and has been an effective complement to the large public libraries. But, a single community library has some disadvantages in management, costs and resource. Through establishing the community libraries alliance based on network, those problem can be effectively solved. However there is a big flaw in the community libraries alliance based on client-server model. Therefore the basic characteristics of cloud computing technology is introduced, and the community library alliance based on cloud computing needs to be analysed in detail. As a relatively new network model, cloud computing has obvious advantage compared with the common client-server model.It has been the field of IT and information concern and strong development. Also, as a new technology, the information security and other issues in it need to be further examined.

REFERENCES

- *http://en.wikipedia.org/wiki/Cloud_computing*
- Mills, Elinor (2009-01-27). *"Cloud computing security forecast: Clear skies"*. CNET News. Retrieved 2010-08-22.
- David Perera (2012-07-12). *"The real obstacle to federal cloud computing"*. FierceGovernmentIT. Retrieved 2012-12-15.
- *"Top 10 Reasons why Startups should Consider Cloud"*. Cloudstory.in. 2012-09-05. Retrieved 2012-12-15.
- *"BMC Service Catalog Enforces Workload Location"*. eweek.com. 2011-08-02. Retrieved 2013-03-10.
- *"HP's Turn-Key Private Cloud - Application Development*

Trends". Adtmag.com. 2010-08-30. Retrieved 2012-12-15.

- Babcock, Charles (2011-06-03). *"RightScale Launches App Store For Infrastructure - Cloud-computing"*. Informationweek.com. Retrieved 2012-12-15.
- *"Red Hat launches hybrid cloud management software - Open Source"*. Techworld. 2012-06-06. Retrieved 2012-12-15.
- Brown, Rodney (April 10, 2012). *"Spinning up the instant cloud"*. CloudEcosystem.

6

Use of Information and Reference Sources for Preparation of Competitive Exams: A Users Survey

Bhupendra Ratha
Lecturer, School of LIS, Devi Ahilya University, Indore (M.P.).
GHS Naidu
Librarian, Central Library, Devi Ahilya University, Indore (M.P.).
Sukhlal Aske
MPhil in LIS Student, School of LIS, Devi Ahilya University, Indore (M.P.).

ABSTRACT

The paper reveals that the users of Central Library, Devi Ahilya University, Indore use the information and reference sources for preparation of competitive exams. In which the study examined the use of information and reference sources, spending time, most preferred language, magazine, newspaper etc. for preparation of competitive exams by the users in Center Library, DAVV, Indore. The study also found that the users use the e-resources or not for the preparation of competitive exams. In the very last the study suggested to the librarian and library staff to improve the library services for the preparation of competition exam and also suggested to the users for making a coordination with the librarian and library staff to improve the same services.

Keywords : Competitive exams, Information sources, Reference sources, E-resources, Central Library.

1. INTRODUCTION

Competitive examinations in India has played an important role in national integration by bringing candidates from different societies under one roof to applied for same job. Competitive exams have become a strict and perfect standard for courses in our country. Competitive exams are a reality for the thousands of students who appear in them every year. In such a situation, everyone wants to be successful. Success in these exams brings enormous credit and self-assurance to the individuals, besides giving them a clear and certain break into their career. However, seats are limited in numbers and everybody who appears cannot be selected. But it does not mean that those who are rejected do not deserve training in these courses. It only means that there are some problems like lack of guidance, lack of information and references source, library facilities etc. The library plays an important role in the success of selectors in competitive exams. The Central Library, DAVV also provides the facility of special membership for competition exams. The present study covered the facilities providing by the Central Library, DAVV for users who are appearing the upcoming competitive exams and also analyzed the users of libraries are satisfied or not satisfied by the collection of library for the preparation of competitive exams.

2. REVIEW OF LITERATURE

Bird, G and Heekin, J M (1994).[1] His study presented the results of a survey conducted over the summer of 1992 on the use of information sources by professionals in the field of aging. In particular, factors affecting the use of electronic information sources were investigated. **Ugah, Akobundu Dike (2011)**[2] From the findings of this study, it has been established that information sources in the university library were inadequate in size, and are not of high quality in terms of the needs of the users. The findings from the study also reveal significant relationships between the size and quality and the use of library services, and that these information sources variables to large extent influence the use of library services. **Reddy, Shankar (2010)**[3] his study reveals that the library is used regularly by the population of scholars, while there are significant levels of use and satisfaction, scholars also clearly expressed the desire for more journals and for access to electronic journals. **Kumari, A. H. and Talwar, Y .G. (2011)**[4] The study presented a comparative analysis of reference collection in university libraries with its number of users. It also found that there is need of strengthen the collection of almanacs, maps, atlases, gazetteers, indexing, abstracting and statistical sources in all the university libraries.

3. OBJECTIVES

The followings are objectives of the study;

1. To determine the usefulness of collection in the central library of DAVV for competition exams.
2. To determine the language preferences for preparation of competition exams in the central library of DAVV.
3. To determine the spending time in central library of DAVV for preparation of competition exams.
4. To determine the preferences of current sources for competition exams.
5. To determine the preferences of Hindi and English magazines for preparation of competition exams.
6. To determine the preferences of Hindi or English

newspapers for preparation of competition exams.

4. HYPOTHESES

The hypotheses of the study are as follows;

1. There is no significant difference between information and reference sources for the preparation of competition exams.
2. There is no significant difference between Hindi and English language for the preparation of competition exams.
3. There is no significant difference between printed and e–resources for the preparation of competition exams.

5. SAMPLING AND METHODOLOGY

The scope of study is very limited. It covered the users of Central Library, DAVV, Indore. The total number of population is 965 users, in which the study taken 100 (10% approximately) users for survey. The study is used survey method. A well-structured questionnaire was designed and used for collecting the primary data. The 100 questionnaires were disseminated to the users from the Central Library, Devi Ahilya University, Indore. Therefore, all the questionnaires were returned and used for this study. On the basis of returned questionnaires input the data in excel sheet after that analyzed the data according to different point of views and presented in the tabular and graphical form as well as described it.

6. DATA ANALYSIS AND INTERPRETATION:

Table 1. Use of University Library

No.	Category	Response	Percentage
1	Yes	100	100%
2	No	0	0%
	Total	100	100%

The above table reveals that all the 100 (100%) users are using the university Libraries for their study.

Table 2. Preparation of Competition Exams

No.	Category	Response	Percentage
1	Yes	95	95%
2	No	5	5%
	Total	100	100%

The above table represents that 95 (95%) users use the central library for preparing the different competition exams while 5(5%) users do not use the central library for preparation of competition exams.

Table 3: Types of Competition Exams

No.	Category	Response	Percentage
1	UPSC	11	10.7%
2	MPPSC	46	44.7%
3	SSC	7	6.8%
4	Banking	23	22.3%
5	All of the above	9	8.7%
6	other	7	6.8%
	Total	103	100%

The above table and graph show that the users of central library do preparation of different types of competitive exams. In which 46(44%) users do preparation for MPPSC exams followed by 23 (22%) users for Banking, 11(11%) users for UPSC, 7(7%) user for SSC, 9(9%) users for all of the above exams, while 7(7%) users for other competition exams.

From the below table and graph the study concluded that 35(37%) users has given competition exam only one time followed by 27(28%) users two times, 10(11%) users three times and 23(24%) users four times.

Table 4. Attempt Competitive Exams

No.	Category	Response	Percentage
1	One	35	37%
2	Two	27	28%
3	Three	10	11%
4	Four	23	24%

Table 5. Spending Time for Competition Exams in CL

No.	Category	Response	Percentage
1	1 hour	12	13%
2	2 hour	34	36%
3	3 Hour	14	15%
4	More than 3 hour	35	36%
	Total	95	100%

The table displays that the spending time in central library for preparation of competition exams by users. In which 35(36%) users spend more than 3 hours per day followed by 34(36%) users spend 2 hours ,14(15%) 3 hours and 12(13%) only 1 hour.

Table 6. Use of Information Source

No.	Category	Response	Percentage
1	Yes	87	92%
2	No	8	8%
	Total	95	100%

The above table and graph expose that how many users use the information source for preparation of competition exams. The 87 (92%) users use the information sources but 8 (8%) users do not use.

Table 7. Types of Information Sources

No.	Category	Response	Percentage
1	Textbooks	30	26%
2	Reports	4	3%
3	Journals	13	11%
4	Magazines	32	29%
5	All types of source	30	26%
6	Other source	6	5%
	Total	115	100%

The above table and graph show that the users of central library use the different types of information source for preparation of competition exams. In which 32 (28%) users read the magazines for preparation of competition exams, followed by 30 (26%) users read textbooks, 30 (26%) users read all the types of sources, 13 (11%) users read journals, 6 (5%) users read other sources and 4 (3%) users read Reports.

Table 8. Use of Reference Sources

No.	Category	Response	Percentage
1	Yes	85	89%
2	No	10	11%
	Total	95	100%

The above table and graph expose that how many users use the information source for preparation of competition exams. The 85 (89%) users use the information sources but 10 (11 %) users do not use.

The below table and graph show that the users of central library read the reference sources for preparation of competition exams. In which 46(32%) users read the yearbooks for preparation of competition exams, followed by 31(22%) users to encyclopedia, 30(18%) users to dictionary, 12(8%) users to other source, 10(7%) users to map, 10(7%) users to globe and 7(5%) users to biography.

Table 9. Types of Reference Sources

No.	Category	Response	Percentage
1	Dictionary	26	18%
2	Encyclopedia	31	22%
3	Yearbook	46	32%
4	Map	10	7%
5	Globe	10	7%
6	Biography	7	5%
7	Other source	12	8%
	Total	142	100%

Table 10. Currents Sources for Preparation of Competitive Exams

No.	Category	Response	Percentage
1	Magazines	19	17%
2	Newspapers	46	39%
3	Personal communication	4	3%
4	Internet /search engines	19	17%
5	All of the above	24	21%
6	Other source	3	3%
	Total	115	100%

The above table and graph display that which current sources are using by the users of central library to getting up-to-date information. In which 46(39%) users use the newspaper to getting up-to-date information, followed by 24(21%) users use all types of current sources, 19(17%) users magazines, 19(17%) users Internet /search engines, 4(3%) users personal communication, 3(3%) users other currents sources use for preparation of competitive exams.

Table 11. Most Preferred Hindi magazine

No.	Category	Response	Percentage
1	Pratiyogita Darpan	58	62%
2	Pratiyogita Kiran	14	15%
3	Pratiyogita Nirdesika	9	9%
4	India Today	9	9%
5	Ghatana Chakra	5	5%
	Total	95	100%

The above table and graph show that which Hindi magazines mostly prefer by users of central library for competition exams. In which the Pratiyogita Darpan is on the top with 56 (62%) positive responses of the users while Pratiyogita Kiran has 14 (15%), Pratiyogita Nirdeshika and India today 9 (9%) and Ghatna Chakra 5 (6%) responses of the users.

Table 12. Most Preferred English Magazine

No.	Category	Response	Percentage
1	Competition Success	42	44%
2	Chronicle	31	33%
3	India Today	17	18%
4	Civil Service Time	5	5%
	Total	95	100%

The above table and graph present that which English magazines mostly prefer by the users of central library for the preparation of competitive exams, in which the competition success is leading with 42(44%) responses followed by the chronicle has 31(33%), India Today 17(18%) and Civil Service Time 5(5%).responses of the users.

Table 13. Most Preferred Hindi Newspaper

No.	Category	Response	Percentage
1	Dainik Bhaskar	48	51%
2	Nai Duniya	20	21%
3	Patrika	12	13%
4	Raj Express	6	6%
5	Peoples Samchar	3	3%
6	Dabang duniya	4	4%
7	Swadesh	2	2%
	Total	95	100%

The above table indicates that which Hindi newspaper mostly prefers by the users of central library for competitive exams. The Dainik Bhaskar is on the top most with 48(51%) responses of the users, followed by Naiduniya has 20(21%) responses, Patrika 12(13%), Raj Express 6(6%), Peoples Samachar 3(3%), Dabang Duniya, 4(4%) and Swadesh 2 (2%) responses of users.

Table 14. Most Preferred English Newspaper

No.	Category	Response	Percentage
1	Hindustan Times	36	38%
2	Free Press	9	9%
3	The Times of India	20	21%
4	DNA	3	3%
5	The Hindu	22	23%
6	The Indian Express	5	5%
	Total	95	100%

The above table shows that which English newspaper mostly prefers by the users of central library for preparation of competition exams. In which the Hindustan times has 36 (38%) responses which is highest, while the Hindu has 22 (23%) responses, The times of India 20 (21%), free press 9 (10%), the Indian express 5 (5%) and DNA 3 (3%).

Table 15. Most Preferred Language in Information Sources

No.	Category	Response	Percentage
1	Hindi	21	22%
2	English	20	21%
3	Both Hindi and English	54	57%
4	Other	0	0%
	Total	95	100%

The above table and graph show that which language mostly prefers by the users of central library for preparation of competition exams. In which 54(57%) users prefer both Hindi and English Languages followed by 21(22%) users only Hindi Language and 20(21%) users only English Language.

Table 16. Preference for Print v/s Electronic Resources

No.	Category	Response	Percentage
1	Print Resources	63	66%
2	E-Resources	32	34%
	Total	95	100%

The above table indicates that the 63 (66%) users mostly prefer to print resources for preparation of competition exams while left 32 (34%) users prefer to e-resources.

Table 17. Use of e-resource for competitive exams

No.	Category	Response	Percentage
1	Yes	71	75%
2	No	24	25%
	Total	95	100%

The above table reveals that the 71 (75%) users use the e-resources for preparation of competition exams and 24 (25%) users do not use the e-resources for competition exams.

Table 18. Types of Electronic source

No.	Category	Response	Percentage
1	e-books	14	20%
2	e-magazines	40	56%
3	e-journals	01	1%
4	e-newspapers	16	23%
	Total	71	100%

This table displays the mostly preferred e-resources for preparation of competition exams. In which the 40 (56%) users prefer to e-magazines, followed by 16 (23%) e- Newspaper, 14 (20%) e- books and 1 (1%) to e-journals.

Table 19. Collection of Central Library DAVV for Competition Exams

No.	Category	Response	Percentage
1	Excellent	10	11%
2	Good	30	32%
3	Average	50	52%
4	Poor	5	5%
	Total	95	100

The table above and graph show that opinion of the users for information collection for competitive exams in central library DAVV. In which 50(52%) users responded to Average, followed by 30(32%) for Good, 10(11%) for Excellent, 5(5%) for poor collection.

8. FINDINGS:

On the basis of analyzed data the findings are as follows.

1. All the users use the university libraries, in which 95% users use the university libraries for preparation of competition exams.
2. The 44% users use the libraries for preparation of MPPSC exams which is highest.

3. The 37% users have attempted the competitive exams.
4. The 36% users spend more than 3 hours in per day.
5. The 92% users use the information sources for preparation of competition exams in which 28% users read the magazines which is highest
6. The 32% users read the years books for preparation of competition exams.
7. The 40% users read the newspapers for current news
8. The Pratiyogita Darpan mostly prefers by 62% users in Hindi magazines while in English magazines the competition success mostly prefers by 44% users.
9. In Hindi Newspapers, the Dainik Bhaskar mostly prefers by 51% users, while in English Newspapers the Hindustan times prefers by 38% users.
10. The 57% users prefers both English and Hindi languages for preparation of competition exams.
11. The lucent's book for general knowledge mostly prefers by the 52% users.
12. Mostly 66% users prefer the print sources for the preparation of competition exams.
13. The 75% users use the e-resources for preparation of competition exams in which 56% users use the e-magazines for preparation of competition exams.
14. The 52% users responded that the collection of university library is average.

9. TESTING OF HYPOTHESIS

The testing of hypothesis prove that the results of our research. The hypothesis of present study is tested on the basis of findings. These are as follows;

1. "There is no significant difference between

information and reference sources for the preparation of competition exams."

Testing : According to finding of table-6, the 92% users use the information sources while the table-7 shows that 89% users use the reference sources. Thus, the first hypothesis is accepted because there is no significant difference between the use of information and reference sources for competitive exams.

2. "There is no significant difference between the uses of Hindi and English language for the preparation of competition exams."

   Testing : According to findings of table-15, the 57% users prefer both English and Hindi language for preparation of competition exams even as left 22% prefer to only Hindi and 21% prefer to only English. Thus, the second hypothesis is accepted because there is no significant difference between the use of Hindi and English language for the preparation of competition exams.

3. "There is no significant difference between printed and e–resources for the preparation of competition exams".

   Testing : According to findings of table-16, the 66% users prefer the print resources for preparation of competition exams while left 34% prefer e-resources. Thus, the third hypothesis is rejected because there is a big difference between the use of printed and electronic resources for the preparation of competition exams.

10. SUGGESTIONS

1. The numbers of books must be increased in university library.
2. The update edition of books must be purchased in Central Library.

3. All the types of information sources related with competition exams should available in library.
4. The collection related to the competition exams should be arranged in well manner.
5. A separate section should be made for the reading and studying of competition exams with all the facilities like collection, seating, water etc.
6. The employees should guide to the arrangement of information and reference sources.
7. The searching system should upgrade like TLLS.
8. The librarian should organize the motivational lectures or programs related to competency skills of users.
9. The library should provide the e-resource for the competition exams.

11. CONCLUSION

In the very last after the analysis, interpretation of data and findings the study gives the report that the facilities of Central Library for the preparation of competition exams are good but the library can more improve if apply all the suggestions of the study. To the improvement of the facilities of library for competition exams the librarian, library staff and users must make coordination. The users can expose their needs in front of librarian and library staff. The library staff should fulfill the users need.

REFERENCES

- Bird G and Heekin J M. Survey on the use of information sources in the field of aging. *Bull Med Library Assoc.* 82(1) (1994) 30-35.
- Ugah, Akobundu Dike. Size and Quality of Information Sources and the Use of Library Services in a University Library. *Nigeria: Michael Okpara University of Agriculture.* (2011).
- Available at *http://www.webpages.uidaho.edu/~mbolin/*

ugah8.htm

- Shankar, Reddy. Use of Information Sources by Research Scholars: A Case Study. *Gulbarga University* (2010)
- http://digitalcommons.unl.edu/cgi/viewcontent.cgi?article=1322&cont ext = libphilprac
- H, A. Kumari and Talwar, V.G. Reference sources collection in university libraries of Karnataka: A study. *Annals of library and information studies.* 58 (2)(2011) 93-99

7

Future Development of LIS Services in E & M Learning Technology

Durga Prasad
Librarian, at CentralDigital Library,
Shree Ganapti Instituteof Technology Ghaziabad

Prem Prakash Sati
Dy. Librarian, CentralLibrary, University of
Petroleum & Energy Studies Dehradun

ABSTRACT

Mobile learning is new and modern confection education field. It is currently difficult to define, conceptualize and discuss. It could perhaps be a wholly new and distinct educational format, needing to set its own standards and expectations. Mobile learning has becomes anther very important complement to the traditional ways of learning after digital learning. The development of the third generation mobile communication technology 3G provides a more adequate technical basis for mobile learning. The integrated objective of m-learning and e-learning is to explore and to accumulate useful knowledge over and above faster coping, searching and to distributing. The present paper discusses in E-learning & M- learning, its needs of e-learning modules, forms, M-learning technologies, components, motivating factors, virtual communication tools, M-learning development, advantages and disadvantage, role of librarians in M-learning technologies and future developments.

Keywords : E-learning, Components, Virtual Communication, M-learning Tool, M-learning Developments, M-learning Technology.

INTRODUCTION

New wave and Information Communication and Technology (ICT) provide computer enhanced learning process which is commonly known as e-learning is a growing and dynamic environment which has given a new shape to higher education besides classroom teaching. E-learning are now the global scenario providing learning facilities in e-mode to such learning programme in which learning and also the course content is delivered to learners electronically though CD ROM, DVD, INTERNET and on-line *E-learning* has emerged as one of the most interactive, effective and revolutionary technologies of education in which the learner and learning providers remain connected with each other via email, video conferencing, discussions forums, instant messages and chat room etc. E-learning has been emerged as the most powerful system of making information, instructional content and learning experiences accessible at learner's computer though electronic technology. Historical Trace out of e-learning- The e-learning is the extension of distance education learning in ICT era, which enables learners and teachers to engage in synchronous as well as asynchronous interaction across space, time and their own pace.

CONCEPTS OF E-LEARNING

In simple terms learning though Internet technology is known as e-learning. 'E-learning is the use of new multimedia technologies and the internet to improve the quality of learning by facilitating access to resources and services as well as remote exchanges and collaboration.' 'E-learning is the delivery of education, which includes activities related to instruction, teaching and learning though various electronic media, such as internet, intranet, extranet, satellite television, video/audio tape or CD ROM.' 'E-learning is pedagogy empowered by digital technology.' Thus, e-learning is interactive learning though digital technologies.'

WHAT IS E-LEARNING?

E-learning is approach to facilitate and enhance learning though both computer and communication technology. Such device can include personal computers, CD-ROMs, Digital Television, PDAs and Mobil Phones. Communication Technology enables the use of the Internet- Mail, Discussion forums, collaborative softer and real learning system.

COMPONENTS OF E-LEARNING

Following are the popular and common e-learning components

- Learning Management system or Learning content Management system.
- Content.
- Collaboration.
- Testing and assessment.
- Skill & Competence.
- E- Commerce.
- Internet video based service.

E-LEARNING SOFTWARE

There are many software available for e-learning. Here I quote some open source & commercial e-learning software.

OPEN SOURCE SOFTWARE

- Atutor

- DeceboLMS
- Dokes
- Internet
- Word Circle
- Site@schools

COMMERCIAL SOFTWARE

- Blackboard
- eCOllege
- Inquisiq
- Grade point
- Learn eXact
- Web CT

NEED FOR E-LEARNING

Today, the information needs of the users have increased enormously so much that no single library on its own can meet their needs. This has necessitated the need for effective linkages and co-operation between libraries and information centers for sharing of available resource & information through network services. Network e-mail, online access, use of CD-Rom, software and hardware system etc. are now being used for resource sharing.The Swami Vivekananda says about education and library' "Education is not information that is put into your brain and runs riot there undigested all your life. You have more education they any man who has got by heart a whole library. If education were identical with information the libraries would be the greatest in the world."

MOTIVATING FACTORS FOR E-LEARNING

- Due to globalization of business, it is essential to bring employees together at the same time; it is possible through e-learning.

- Corporate sector wants enhancement in their competitiveness by training to manpower.
- Employees want to enhance their learning opportunities.
- Wide spread proliferation of information technology has enable the employees to have access to Internet.

MOBILE-LEARNING (M-LEARNING) TECHNOLOGY

Mobile learning through the use of wire mobile technology allows anyone to access information and learning materials from anywhere and at anytime as a result learner have control of when they want to learn and from which location they want to learn. Also all human have right to access learning materials and information to improve their quality of life regardless of where they live, their status and their culture. mobile learning, through the use of mobile technology, will allow citizens of the world to access learning materials and information from anywhere and at anytime. Learners will not have to wait for a certain time to learn or to a certain place to learn. With mobile learning, learners will be empowered since they can learn whenever and wherever they want. Also, learners do not have to learn what is prescribed to them. They can use the wireless mobile technology for formal and informal learning where they can access additional and personalized learning materials from the internet or host organization. Teacher can use the mobile technology to access training material and information when they need it for just-in-time training just-in-time learning encourages high level learning since learner's access and applies the information right away rather than learns the information and then applies the information at a later time. Trainer are empowered since they accuse the mobile technology to communicate with learned from anywhere and at anytime.

BASIC SIP COMMANDS:

- **INVITE :** Initiates a session. This method includes information about the calling and called users and the type of media that is to be exchanged.
- **ACK :** Sent by the client who sends the INVITE? ACK is sent to confirm that the session is established. Media can then be exchanged.
- **BYE :** Terminates a session .This method can be sent by either user.
- **CANCEL :** Terminates a pending request, such as an outstanding INVITE. After a session is established a BYE method needs to be used terminate the session.
- **OPTIONS :** Queries the capabilities of the server or other devices. It can be used to check media capabilities before issuing an INVITE.
- **REGISTER :** Used by a client to login and register its address with a SIP registrar server.

M-LEARNING TOOLS USED

SIP : SIP is an application- layer control protocol that can establish, modify, and terminate multimedia sessions (conference) such as Internet telephony calls. SIP can also invite participants to already existing sessions, such as multicast conference. Normally SIP uses UDP and TCP port 5061 for SSL communication. SIP protocol is very similar to HTTP, so if you have some knowledge about HTTP, then it is easy to learn SIP. SIP doesn't transfer session data like audio, video. RTP (Real Time Protocol) is used for that, SIP just helps to open RTP streams.

ROLE OF LIBRARIANS IN M-LEARNING

The following are the role the librarian in M-learning

- M-learning nowadays becomes the order of the day

and it is being used to impart education.

- Librarians are the information intermediaries who can help the users in making use of e-resources
- The librarians need to be made aware of the internet and the resources available therein and how to make efficient use of them.
- The idea behind m-learning module is to train both the librarians as well as the users regarding the efficient use of e-resources.
- The emphasis is on the resources related to librarianship in addition to general topics of interest.

M-LEARNING TECHNOLOGIES

M-learning technologies used to support different educational configurations in terms of place and time video conferencing for example, is a same time. Different place technology. Whereas e-mail can support different time, different place.

The Following figure shows technologies used in m-learning and their advantage.

Different Place	**Synchronous interaction** Group interactive video Desktop interactive video Chat sessions Audio conferencing Collaborative groupware whiteboard	**Asynchronous interaction** Online discussion forums E-mail Voice mail Video mail Video on demand web casting collaborative document editing
Same Place	**Classroom-based instruction** Black boards Teaching theater In-class lab and groupware Presentation tools	**Shared use** Laboratory assignments Self-paced programmes in central facility

ISSUES IN M-LEARNING TODAY

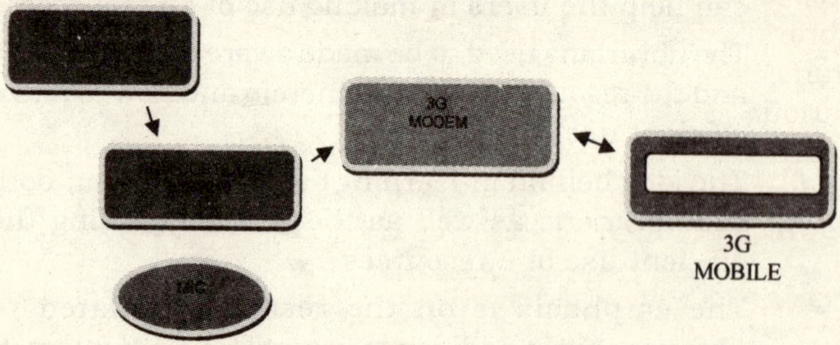

Fig. 1. Mobile learning using 3G Technology

Today M-learning is considered as alternative tools of empowering knowledge and skills. It is also treated as alternative means for classroom teaching. Now with the help of it is possible to deliver the information with highest degree of precision which is not possible with traditional skills. It has overcome several constraints of traditional system. But still there are some issues such as the Above Figure 1.

DEVELOPING LIBRARY SERVICES IN M-LEARNING ENVIRONMENT

Repid spread of information communication technologies, Recent reduction in technology costs and increasing PC awareness in learner are very much attractive. Many libraries are in the process of delivering the information services and resources through the online chat rooms, e-mail services, list serves, or fee online databases and reference services, teleconferencing and toll free numbers.

ACCESS TO INFORMATION RESOURCES

Student at remote sites must get the information resources supporting their learning. Computer search services should be extended with full text document delivery. Library should provide full text documents. In a step ahead the e-learning the library can setup the digital library. Digital library will break all the barriers of data transfer. It can store a large amount of information in various forms i.e., text, audio, video, graphic material. Learners can make effective search for the information in digital libraries with sophisticated search engines and download into his or her system.

CONSULTATION SERVICES

Consultation can be conducted through e-mail, toll free telephone services, pre –packged mail out information or scheduled remote site visits.

REFERENCES SERVICES

Electronically references on the inter is gaining more popularity reference librarian In the distance education programme learner can use forms to make research queries with the ready reference services in the form frequently asked question (FAQ) is most convenient for the learner.

INTER-LIBRARY LONE AND CONSORTIA SHARING

Today there is one or the form of network or cooperation is existing in the form of associations or consortia. Such as INFLIBNET, DELNET, CALIBNET etc. further each of the member library possess the computer, online systems and network. The effective electronic transmissions of document demand helps quicker inter library loan and information services.

INSTRUCTION AND TRAINING

One of the main problem in e-learning system that learner should have sufficient knowledge and skills of usage of the information technology in the web based education require much training as the e-learning involves different types of multimedia files.

INTERACTION

There is a lack interaction between learner and subject specialist. It may possible for subject expert availability. But teacher may be possible to access via e-mail. Some time face interaction can be made possible through online conferencing. E-learning designer should need to increase the interactivity.

SPEED OF NETWORK

To access the learning material it is very much required to connect internet. As e-learning involves multimedia file, higher speed of network with sufficient bandwidth is required.

BUDGETARY SUPPORT

Considerable infrastructure such as hardware, software and manpower requires heavy investment. Organization who wants to start e-learning system should have enough funding.

QUALITY OF THE SERVICE

To ensure the higher quality of the services to its user regular survey is required to test the material and they should be repackaged on periodical basis.

COPYRIGHT

Libraries need to distribute copies of the same information to the distance learners. So librarian must be familiar with the sufficient right to acquire intellectual property.

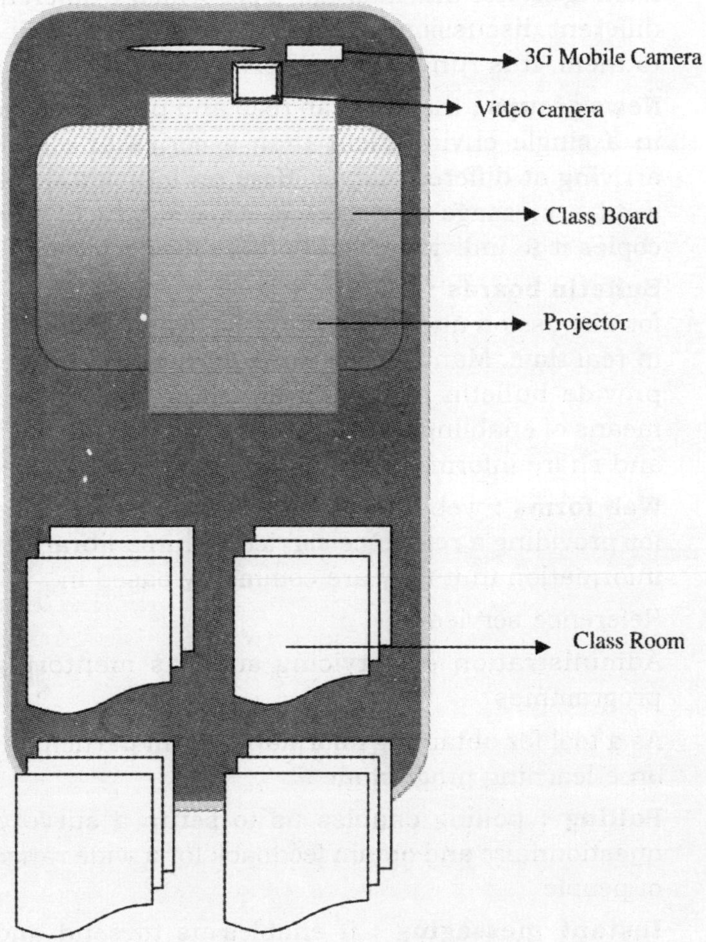

Fig. 2. A live video of classroom on 3G mobile phone

VIRTUAL COMMUNICATION TOOL

- The following tool are they are;
- E-mail; e-mail is used by information workers, librarian and other for formal and learning and teaching activities
- Mailing list; it is possible to send e-mail to groups using mailing lists. The process is managed by a

hosting service that maintain a list of all the different different discussion list and people who subscribe to them. It is run by a mail server.

- **News groups :** the user can read and post message in a single environment than a series of e-mail arriving at different times. Here an individual will send a message to a central source ,which then copies it to individuals and other news groups.
- **Bulletin boards :** bulletin boards provide a facility for discussion under various topic heading and not in real time. Many library and information services provide bulletin boards within their websites as means of enabling their customers to discuss ideas and share information.
- **Web forms :** web form are often used as a means for providing a reference service within a library or information unit they are commonly based in
- Reference service
- Administration of servicing such as mentoring programmes
- As a tool for obtaining information from participant on e-learning programme
- **Polling :** polling enables us to setup a survey/ questionnaire and obtain feedback for a wide range of people
- **Instant messaging :** it enables us to send and display a message on someone's screen in a matter of seconds. It means the staff who is working on a busy reference or help point may message a colleague with a question and obtain response.
- **Chat or conferencing :** this enables users to hold a live discussion by sending each other short written messages.
- **Internet telephony :** in this tool a user can make calla by using the internet. An individual can make

distance phone calls through the computer and the internet without paying long-distance phone charges.

- **Video conferencing :** it requires specialists and very expensive machines are used in video conferencing.
- **Virtual worlds :** used for e –learning within universities, it is possible to through dimensional virtual world.

ADVANTAGES THE FOLLOWING THE ADVANTAGE OF M-LEANING

- Lower costs
- Time savings
- Flexibility
- Faster response
- Greater effectiveness
- Better competitiveness
- M-learning complements the process and can help reach out the masses.
- M-learning lies in its ability to cover distances.
- The consistency that e-learning provides, e-learning is learning is done at the learners.
- Learning resources can be pace easily developed using a variety of standard packages.
- One can make use of, and link into other resources available on the internet
- Online delivery cheap as there are no printing or distribution costs
- It is easy to track learner activity and progress.
- Electronic learning where the student can access the study modules through web, irrespective of the location, time etc.
- It is interactive and can serve as a substitute for a classroom teaching environment

DISADVANTAGE

- Many people find it daunting, especially at first
- The student and tutor need reliable to a computer and internet.
- The student and tutor need basic information technology skills
- Training is required for both tutor and student
- The development of high-quality learning materials is time consuming and expensive.
- Online tutoring can be more time- consuming than face to face tutoring.
- Learning is a social process and many people enjoy face to face interactions.
- The use of the large virtual learning environments is expensive and may demand additional equipment and specialized staff.
- Some learning environments require state of the art computer and the most update browser
- Blended solutions can be expensive as they may involve the development of expensive online learning resources and providing technology based support as well as face- to face support.

FUTURE DEVELOPMENTS

Automatic Response to question : Problems of learners received, the server should be in accordance with the method of matching.

Browsing questions and answers : Learners though the system should visit the other student's question and corresponding answers, in order to achieve knowledge-sharing with each other to improve.

Sending notification of teaching activities : System should send notification to students when they go out to, so that students can be in touch with the educational institution at any time, replacing a lot of inconvenience.

CONCLUSION

In e-learning process the future libraries will emerge as active bridge between the learning and information. E-learning supporting by digital library is very much significant and critical in Higher education and research. Mobile Technologies are development rapidly, and the functionalities available on mobile devices grow more numerous and complex every day. These technological advancement, coupled with the widespread and ubiquity of mobile technologies to enhance learning and extend educational opportunities. In 3G system, it can be realized between the mobile end user data, audio, video, multimedia communications, which make anytime, any were "ease face to face" communication is possible. Students will be able to carry visual communication with the teachers and enable teachers to guide learning. A thirds generation mobile communication 3Gtechnology has greatly accelerated the convergence of mobile communication and the internet, the communication of mobile communication in the context; 3G communication technology will be widely applied to education. With the practice of in-depth and awareness-raising mobile education will showcase its endless charm.

REFERENCES

1. 3Mtrack & trace solutions, 3M India ltd., Bangalore.
2. Allan & Barbara. E-learning and Teaching in Library & Information Services, 2002, Facet publishing, London.
3. Anandkrishnan, M. "e-learning: substitute or supplement?" paper presented in xx IATLIS national conference, Madras Chennai 21-23 Pp. 123-129.
4. Annandan, C. & Gangatharan, M. 2002, Digital Library: From Technology to Culture 1st Edition, New Delhi: Kanishka Publisher.

5. Ashraf, Tariq. "New Information Environment; a challenge for Librarianship."University news, 41 (19) May 12-18, 2003, 9-15.

6. Desmond, Keegan "The future of learning: from e-learning to m-learning." Information Analyses.2002.11, pp44-65.

7. EUROPEAN COMMISSION. The e-learning action plan: Designing tomorrow's education, 2001. Available in http:www.study mentor.com/study mentor/.

8. Joshi, Vinod "e-learning to the wisdom" the Hindu October 15.2003.

9. Keegan, Desmond, "the future of learning: From e-learning in of m learning" Information Analysis.2002.11, Pp44-65.

10. Kohei Arai, Herman Tolle "Efficiency improvement of e-learning document search engine for mobile browser" International Journal of research and review ın computer science (IJRRCS) Vol.02. No.06; dec.2011, Pp1287-1291.

11. KOOHANG, A. and HARMAN, K. Open Source: A metaphor of learning. Information Science Journal. 8, 2005, p.75-86.

12. NICHOLS, M. E-learning in context, E-Primer Series 2008 Available in : http//akaotearora.ac.nz/download/ng/file/group-661/877-1.....e-learning-in-context pdf.

13. Riggs, D.E "Distance education: rethinkikingpractices, implementing new approaches" collage and research libraries 58, 1997.Pp. 208-209.

14. Sangam S L and Vantal R M "e- learning and libraries in offering LIS education" Paper presented at xx IATLIS national conference, Chennai, 21-23. Nov. Pp. 123-129.

15. Seppala & H .Alamaki, "Mobile learning in teacher training" Journal of computer Assisted learning (2003)19.

16. Srivastava, D.K.- E-learning : A New way of Education, University News 43 (26) 2005,27-3.

17. Supyan Hussin, Mohd Radzi Manap, Zaini Amir & Pramela Krish, " Mobile learning Readiness among Malaysian Students at Higher learning Institute" Asian Social Science; Vol. 08, No. 12; 2012, p276-283.

18. Vathal, R.M.- Introducing Electronic Information Resources through E-learning mechanism. University News 42 (14) (2004) 5-11

19. Why e-learning is so powerful? [www.zdnetindiacom/specials/elarning/]. 2 December 2003.

20. Wu Junqi, Qi Lili, Zhaengbing Hu, "3G Phone-Based mobile learning for improving K-12 Teachers' educational technology in rural area" ,2010 Second International Workshop on education technology and computer Science,P821-825.
21. www.3M.com/us/library
22. www.expresscomputronline.com
23. www.infomedia.co.in
24. www.niceretail.bi2
25. www.rdg.co.in
26. www.rgrhs.ac.in
27. www.thehindu.com.
28. Yazhen Zhang, Jian Li. "Application of 3G-Based mobile learning in teacher training" 2011 Fourth Conference on information and computing, P27-29.

8

Effectiveness of Computerisation in The Libraries of ICSSR Institutes – An Evaluative Study

Shiv Sindhu Chouksey
Librarian, RGPV Bhopal

ABSTRACT

Advancement of technology has made possible to retrieve and storage of Information in digital, optical sources of libraries of ICSSR through computerization. In this study author find the effectiveness of computer application in the field of social science libraries with special reference of ICSSR. The main objective of the study is to know the present status of computerization in terms of:

a. Status of computerization in the libraries of ICSSR.

b. Present status of the use of computers in the libraries of ICSSR.

c. Sources use of data entry for database of the libraries of ICSSR.

d. Status of the computerized library sections in the libraries of ICSSR.

e. Status of responsibility for computerization of the libraries of ICSSR.

It can be concluded that the computerization of the libraries of ICSSR is not too good, though the libraries have all the required system for computerization. There are several causes for that like paucity of funds, financial crunch, lack of skilled personnel, lack of infrastructure, etc. Therefore it is still need to encourage the libraries to take step for computerization.

INTRODUCTION

The service sector is the libraries have crucial role for the development of the society as well as in social science research. It is very difficult for developing countries to set up the state of the art services for all kind of knowledge communication and its management. So that one can seek and find the desire information from its storehouse of knowledge. The pace of technological change in communication & information sectors during the past two decades directly affected development information services. Through computerization of the libraries have universally been recognized but its application is the libraries are still poor.

The use of digital libraries in India is increasing day by day. But due to paucity of funds, computer illiteracy we are unable to enter info digital system is a large way in India. It is well known facts the computer literate in India are still less in number, especially in library and information field. Even after couple of years library automation activities are still is poor state of affairs, library networks are still is their infancy stage.

Indian Institute of Social Science Research (ICSSR) is developed a chain of social Science research Institutes during the last five decades in India. The ICSSR working as a premier national agency for expanding social science research improving its quality and attempting to its utilization in policy formulation. There are 27 ICCSR research institutes is India, located is 15 major states.

Dr. Shiv Sindhu Chouksey, HOD Library, Central

Library Rajiv Gandhi Technical University Bhopal (MP).

OBJECTIVES

1. To know the present status of computerization in the libraries of ICSSR institute.
2. To find out the effectiveness of the computerization is the libraries of ICSSR institutions.

SCOPE & LIMITATION OF THE STUDY

The finding of the study may provide guidelines to ICSSR, Govt. organization, NGO's Planner etc. These findings will also be useful for researchers, policy makers & for all those who are concerned with the same field. The problem is based on the libraries of ICSSR Institute therefore it can be generalized for social science research libraries of India.

The study is purely based on the primary secondary and tertiary sources of information. The study is limited in terms of time and specific geographical area. The study is conducted in the field of social science particularly in the ICSSR institute.

RESEARCH METHODOLOGY

Library professional of ICSSR institute of ICSSR institute library comprises the universe of the study.

A purposive sampling of non-probable sampling framework has been adopted in this study for the selection of library personnel (see table-1).

For a proper spatial coverage the selection of the respondents was made from all 27-research institute of ICSSR from each institute one library professional was selected for the study (Seed fig.1)

The questionnaire method was adopted for the collection at data as the study is concerned with the library automation in libraries of ICSSR. It was essential to make use of observational method to extract.

Information & get in sight into the issues involved. After completion of data collection, the observations, information was systematically classified.

On the basis of filled questionnaire a codebook was prepared & accordingly the entire questionnaires were coded. Coded questionnaire were analyzed is terms of simple percentage.

Table 1. Library Professionals Selected As Repondents

S.No.	Name of the Institutes	No. Of Selected Respondents
1.	IIE PUNE	1
2.	ANSISS PATANA	1
3.	IEG DELHI	1
4.	GIS VARANASI	1
5.	CSDS NEW DELHI	1
6.	IPE HYDERABAD	1
7.	CSS SURAT	1
8.	SPIESR AHAMDABAD	1
9.	GIRD AHAMADBAD	1
10.	CSD NEW DELHI	1
11.	MIDS CHENNAI	1
12.	CDS TRIVENDRUM	1
13.	ISEC BANGLORE	1
14.	CSSS KOLKATTA	1
15.	GIDS LUCKNOW	1
16.	CPR NEW DELHI	1
17.	CMDR DHARWAD	1
18.	CRRID CHANDIGARH	1
19.	GBPSSI ALLAHABAD	1
20.	CESS HYDERABAD	1
21.	CWDS NEW DELHI	1
22.	IDS JAIPUR	1
23.	MPISSR UJJAIN	1
24.	ISID NEW DELHI	1
25.	NKCCDS BHUBNESWAR	1
26.	BANISS MHOW	1
27.	LOKDISC & D GUVAHATI	1
	TOTAL	27

ICSSR STRUCTURE OF SAMPLING FRAME

The ICSSR working as a premier national agency for expanding social science research improving its quality and attempting to its utilization in policy formulation. There are 06 regional centers and 27 ICCSR research institutes sampling/ collection of data from the all the institutes.

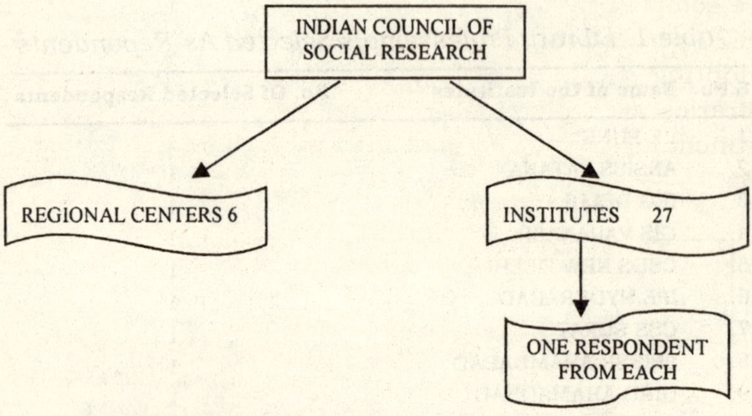

Fig. 1. ICSSR Structure of Sampling Frame

Samples collect form the all the institutes

RESULT AND DISCUSSIONS

We are living an information era. The advancement of technology has make possible to retrieve and storage information in digital optical, audiovisual forms on can browse digital and traditional information in a shorter time by using latest information technology thus the use of computer technology in the libraries has become panacea for the libraries.

STATUS OF COMPUTERIZATION OF THE LIBRARIES

The status of computerization can be seen in the below mention table No.2.

Table 2. Status of computerization of the libraries

S.No.	Computerized Categories	Percentage
1.	Yes	40.90
2.	Partially	40.90
3	No	18.20

Table 2 reveals that 40.90 percent libraries of ICSSR are computerized while 40.90 percent are partially and 18.20 percent are non-computerized. The reason for not adopting the latest information technology it's their libraries are different like paucity of funds, financial crunch, lack of skilled personnel, lack of infrastructure etc.

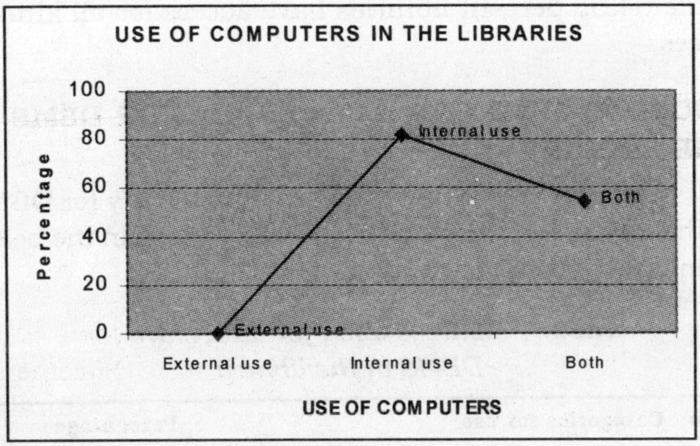

Fig. 2. Statuses for the Use of Computers in the Libraries

STATUSES OF USE OF COMPUTERS IN THE LIBRARIES

The status of use of computers can be seen in the below mention table No. 3.

Table 3. Statuses of Use of Computers in the Libraries

S.No.	Categories for use	Percentage
1.	External use	0.09
2.	Internal use	81.82
3	Both	54.55

There is much difference between the use and availability of computer. it is not necessary that computers available in libraries are always in proper use. It may be possible that its use restricted for faculties or outside users or both. Table 3 indicate that only 9.09 percents libraries of ICSSR allowed to use the computers for external users where as 81.82 percent of the libraries permit only for their (internal users) faculty members while 54.55 percent libraries have access for all kind of users.

SOURCES USED FOR DATA ENTRY FOR DBMS IN THE LIBRARY

The status of Sources used for data entry for DBMS in the library for computerization can be seen in the below mention table No.4.

Table 4. Sources used for data entry for DBMS in the library

S.No.	Categories for use	Percentage
1.	Existing library catalogue	41.00
2.	Accession Register	27.27
3.	Document itself	41.00
4.	Union Catalogue	00.00
5.	MARC of other library	4.55
6.	Bibliographic data base	13.64
7.	Data exchange	00.00
8.	Downloading	4.55
9.	Uploading	4.55
10.	Retrospective conversion	9.00

Data in table 4 indicate that maximum 41% of libraries use existing library catalogue & document itself for the data entry of books & journals for the DBMS, while 27% use accession register, while union catalogue and data exchange does not used in any libraries.

STATUS OF THE COMPUTERISED SECTION IN THE LIBRARIES

The status of the computerized section in the libraries can be seen in the below mention table No.5.

Table 5. Status of the Computerised Section in the Libraries

S.No.	Sections	Percentage
1.	Acquisition	27.27
2.	Processing	.09
3.	Reference	27.72
4	Periodical	45.45
5.	Cataloguing	50.00
6.	Technical	13.64
7.	Circulation	27.72
8.	Documentation	45.45
9.	Administration	18.18
10.	Accounts	13.64

Thus 5 depict the status of computerized section in the libraries. It shows that maximum 50% of the surveyed libraries has computerized cataloging sections 45.45, 27.27, 27.27 and 18.18 percent of libraries has periodical & documentation, circulation & references, Acquisition, administration computerized section respectively.

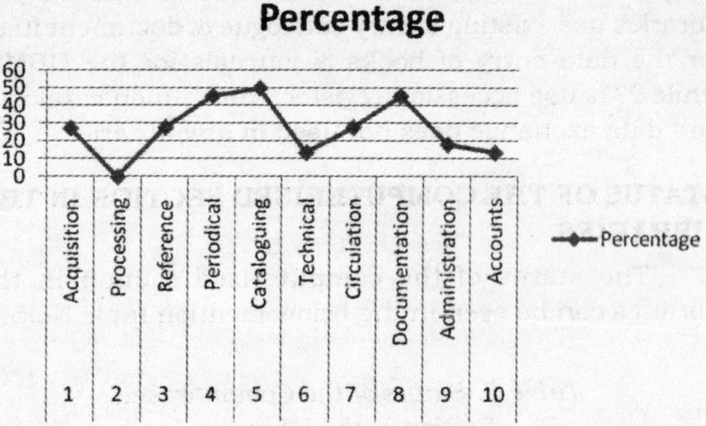

Thus it can be predicated that periodical cataloguing and documentation sections are computerized in most of the libraries.

STATUS OF RESPONSIBILITY FOR COMPUTERISATION OF LIBRARIES

The status of responsibility for computerization of libraries can be seen in the below mention table No.6.

Table 6. Status of Responsibility for Computerisation of Libraries

S.No	Categories (In charge)	Percentage
1.	Librarian	72.27
2.	IT Expert	9.09
3.	No Response	27.72

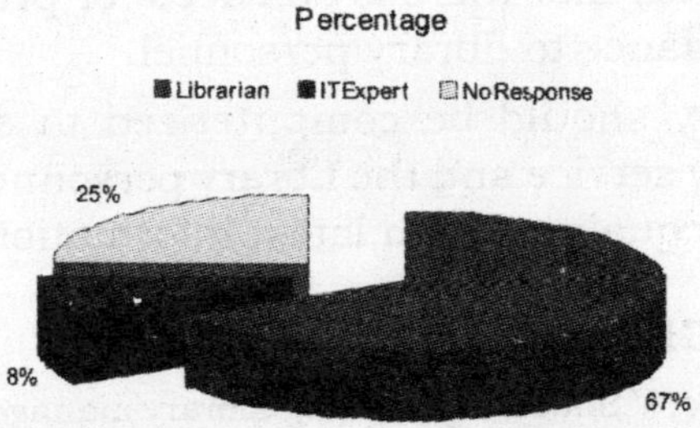

Fig. 6. Status of Responsibility for Computerisation of Libraries

Table 6 shows the status of the responsibility for computerization of the libraries. It depicts that 72.27 percent of respondents state that librarian is the charge for the computerization of the libraries, 9.09 percent respondents mentioned that librarian is the in charge but in consultation with the IT EXPERT; so it is obvious that the librarian is responsible for the computerization of the library provided infrastructure facilities given to them.

CONCLUSION

1. It can be concluded that the computerization of the libraries of ICSSR is not too good, though the libraries have all the required system for computerization. There are several causes for that like paucity of funds, financial crunch, lack of skilled personnel, lack of infrastructure, etc. Therefore it is still need to encourage the libraries to take step for computerization.
2. Most of the libraries are using either existing library catalogue or document itself for creation of DBMS for this physical form of the books should be used for data entry purposes. This will reduce the physical labor for stock verification of the libraries.
3. Periodical, Cataloguing and documentation sections are computerized in most of the libraries. This

indicates that there is still need for proper training & guidance to library personnel.

4. Library should be computerized to enhance the library service and the library personnel need to be well acquainted with latest information.

REFERENCE

- Subbarao, V Shashikala (1999), Library management through automation and net working, Allied, Bombay.
- Bajpai S.K. (1999) Preservation and management of Library collection, Ess Ess, New Delhi.
- Nair, Raman R (1999), Computer application of library and information system Ess Ess New Delhi
- Dalai B.K. & Ramesh D.B. (1999), A tool for evaluation of special library, A case study, Annals of library Science & Documentation, 41(3) 1994, P. 116-120 Kumar Ranjeet (1999) Research methodology, A step guide for beginners, sage, New Delhi.
- Prasad Y V Shiv, Software Requirements for library automation library and Information, Vstas in library, information system and network : Festschrift to Professor S M Tripathi/ Edited M V Venugopal, G Narasimha Murthy, M Sankara Reddy and J N Gautam.Y K Pub., Agra, 1999.

9

Traditional Librarianship to E-Librarianship: Role of Academic Librarian in the E-Learning Environment: Challenges and Issues

Jitendra Shrivastava
Asst. Professor, Dept. of Library & Information Science
Maharani Laxmibai Govt.College of Excellence, Gwalior (M.P.)

Manoj Tiwari
Reseach Scholar, Deptt of Library & Inf Sc
MLB Govt College of Excellence,Gwalior (M.P.)

Nidhi S. Tiwari
Reseach Scholar, Deptt of Library & Inf Sc
MLB Govt College of Excellence,Gwalior (M.P.)

ABSTRACT

As the information technologies are changing day-today and growing at a tremendous speed, the knowledge society is becoming more complex, competitive and dependent on technological changes and information explosion. The need for e-information services to the users are also growing and becoming very essential. The impact of web based e-learning and teaching environment has influenced every facet of library and information services in academic libraries and providing new opportunities and challenges to the library professional for involvement in the knowledge based society including electronic and multimedia publishing, Internet based-information services, global networking, web based digital resources etc. Librarians are charged with selecting and organizing resources and instructing patrons on how to locate and use these, and preserving information regardless of format or technology. The information revolution and the knowledge that is available on the Web have created new challenges to these traditional professional ethics. The emerging challenges of acquiring and providing access to electronic knowledge resources require librarians to change their role from traditional librarian to information scientist by learning and applying new skills to understand the evolving technologies to manage and provide quality on-line information service to the knowledge society. So the vision of the future academic library professional must be to create a World Class Networked Global Library and Information Centre to provide timely web based quality information service to the user in time in the e-learning environment. The future visions need for changes in academic libraries, trends and challenges before the library professional in the e-learning environment and the various changing roles of the academic library professional also have been discussed in this paper

Keywords: Information Technology, academic Library Professional, Web Technology, Technology challenges, e-resources, e-learning environment.

INTRODUCTION

The information atmosphere around the world is changing every minute and growing at a tremendous speed due to the emergence of the web based Information and Communication Technologies (ICT), globalization of networks and Internet. Hence ensuring and organizing access to educational materials in the electronic environment is an important factor in determining realistic requests for development and advancement of education. The information revolution and the pervasive thinking that everything is available on the Web have created new challenges to the traditional library professional ethics. Acquiring and providing access to electronic knowledge resources require library professional to change their role from traditional librarian to information scientist by learning and applying new skills to understand the evolving technologies to manage and provide quality on-line information service to the patrons of the knowledge society. Since, almost all the educational institutions, organizations, universities and academic associations have created their own websites with the digital repositories on Internet, the global networked environment has paved the way and opportunity to literacy. The impact of web based e-learning and teaching environment has influenced very much on every facets of library and information services in Academic Libraries and providing new opportunities and challenges to the library professionals.

OBJECTIVE

The objectives of this paper are given below:

1. The primary objective of this paper is to analyze and explore the changing vision and the roles of future academic library professionals accordingly to meet the changes and challenges in the e-learning environment.
2. To document the various changes and challenges evolved before the academic library professional in the e-learning environment
3. To define and explain the concept of e-literacy and digital learning environment in academic institutions which changes the role of library professional to the real situation.
4. To discuss about the various skills needed for the library professional to meet the present online and digital needs of the user.

VISIONS OF THE FUTURE ACADEMIC LIBRARY PROFESSIONALS

Technology will continue to change, and libraries and librarians have to use the changing technology to provide the best access and service to their patrons. Electronic information creates challenges for the library community at its very foundation, moving it away from the traditional paper-and-print format to an ethereal world of circuits and connectivity. The library is no longer defined simply as a building or a physical repository that houses information. So the essential future vision of the academic library professional to achieve the necessary information transformation and to face the digital information needs of the user should concentrate on the followings:

- The vision of the future academic library professional must be to create a World Class Networked Global Library and Information Centre to provide web based quality information service to the user in time in the e-learning environment.
- The librarians must change the library environment as pathways to high quality information in a variety of electronic media and information sources.
- Library professional must assert their evolving roles in more pro-active ways, both in the context of their academic institutions and in the context of increasing competitive markets for information dissemination and retrieval.
- *The vision for the21st Century librarians*must offer electronic teaching and learning both to guide and beckon the library profession as education leaders. They should shape the library programme and serve as a tool for library media specialists to use to shape the learning of students in the academic institutions.

REVIEW OF EARLIER LITERATURE ON CHALLENGING ROLES OF LIBRARIANS IN THE E-LEARNING ENVIRONMENT

The concept of a digital library and its usages for faculty at the university and the changing role of librarians in creating and managing digital libraries are described by Joseph Janes, Assistant Professor at the University of Washington Information School. He also presented a case study of the Internet Public Library <*http://www.ipl.org/*> developed between 1994 and 1995 by the then School of Information and Library Studies at the University of Michigan which illustrated how a digital library can support education.

Christine Dugdale in her presentation on Electronic Library System which offers access to electronic reservation systems, current awareness service, has shown how short loan collections can provide access to a great quantity and range of material for a larger distribution of learners6. Bonk (2004), reviews the trends in online e-literacy programmes in colleges and universities both in the United States and around the world, which describe the desire of teachers to empower the learner, the power of future developments such as simulations and virtual world technology in education4. Karen Jurasek says that libraries must uphold professional standards and a commitment to service11. Also he describes that along with its services, resources, and technology, the library is both a physical and virtual space for the 21st century. He also concludes that the academic library professional must develop a virtual electronic learning system to enhance the user's knowledge and to accommodate an increasingly diverse group of users. John McColl's presentation was on virtual learning environments (VLEs) and the aim of his project was to integrate open library resources and closed learning environments. Also he describes that since Virtual Learning Environment contain links to resources, both licensed and free, overlaps with electronic reserve systems, and has a dynamic linking potential with library, librarians should be involved in creating and maintaining VLEs as resource managers in this new environment of web-based courses. Kasperek, Johnson, Fotta, and Craig, found that "...continued involvement with play participants outside the library increased student comfort level both with the library in general and the librarian for their major...[and] that students are more comfortable with librarians once they have the opportunity to get to know them." Kinnie similarly found that increased involvement with faculty outside traditional library responsibilities also improved his subject specialty liaison work. Dewey likewise promotes the embedding of academic librarians into as many campus venues as possible as a way of "advancing colleges' and universities' strategic priorities through constant collaboration" and Gamble argues for the recognized presence of academic librarians on university governance committees, faculty unions, clubs and student activities as legitimate modes for providing university service that ought to be valued and rewarded by library administration.

E-LITERACY/VIRTUAL LEARNING ENVIRONMENTS IN ACADEMIC INSTITUTIONS AND THE FUTURE OF THE ACADEMIC LIBRARIES

E-learning is a means of becoming literate, involving new mechanisms for communication, such as: Computer networks, multimedia, content portals, search engines, electronic libraries, distance learning, and web-enabled classrooms. Different web based applications such as email, real-time conference; Web Cam, etc. are being used as important tools in the process of e-learning. Technological innovations have brought tremendous changes in the whole education process and have led to a paradigm shift from teacher based education to a learner based education system. Developments in the electronic networking frontier have changed the whole dimension of the education system. This has brought a shift from the 'just in cast education' to 'just in time education' system. Internet, another cost-effective solution of reaching out to the learners at a distance, is gaining ground throughout the world. It is acting as a catalyst for change in the education process. It has taken education beyond the classroom and lecture hall into a new era of networked and collaborative learning. Since the aim of e-learning environment in education is to enhance students' learning opportunities by enabling them to partake in global, team based educational projects, in which they directly experience different cultural contexts and access a variety of digital information sources via a range of appropriate Information and communication technology, the future academic library professional should change their role by developing new standards and skills accordingly to meet the future digital information needs of the users. Today almost all the academic institutions, universities and college libraries have been automated by library software and have become connected with Internet, intranet and extranet facilities and through which they are providing access to relevant e-journals and e-books by proxy-server based networks. So the future of the academic library services may be changed accordingly to fulfill the needs of the patrons in the e-learning environment. Libraries have an outstanding potential as the third place, after home and work with learning, inspiration and entertainment. Hence it is very essential to change the environment, structure and interiors of the academic libraries according to the digital information needs of the user and the future library should not have collection storage as its main function. E-learning opportunities must be enabled by the library professionals to the user in global level to access a variety of digital information sources via a range of appropriate World Wide Web technology. E-Learning is a catch-all term that covers a wide range of instructional material that can be delivered on a CD-ROM or DVD, over a local area network (LAN), or on the Internet. It includes Computer-Based Training (CBT), Web-Based Training (WBT), and Electronic Performance Support Systems (EPSS), distance or online learning and online tutorials. The major advantage to students is its easy access. So, providing access to online e-journals and e-books through networks will enhance the self-learning knowledge of the user.

TRENDS AND CHALLENGES BEFORE THE FUTURE ACADEMIC LIBRARY PROFESSIONALS IN THE ELEARNING ENVIRONMENT

The first and foremost challenge before the library professionals to face the future academic needs of the user in the e-learning environment is to provide electronic access to all relevant information and integrate it on networks across the world. The second challenge is to create a new physical library premises with computer network facilities, abandoning the old concept of library as a storehouse, and, the third challenge to future library professionals is to develop new standards and skills for the library profession to meet the user needs in a proactive way. In this e-learning and e-publishing environment, electronic reference services and other support services with various expertise and digital repositories are becoming a must. The most pressing and pervasive issues and challenges that the library and information science professionals face in the present digital era for providing digital information service to the knowledge society are:

i) New generation of learners
ii) Copyright
iii) Privacy/Confidentiality
iv) Online/Virtual crimes and Security
v) Technology challenges

vi) Man power

vii) Collection of digital e-resources

viii) Organizational Structure

ix) Preservation / archiving of digital e-resources

x) Lack of clarity in vision

The New Generation of Learners

Today's students are grown up with latest information and communication technologies. They are coming to higher education with aptitude, knowledge and expectations that have been shaped by the use of the Internet, digital media, and portable communication technologies. Students often begin their search for information with Google or similar commercial or social search engines. The academic library professional must develop a virtual electronic learning system to enhance the student's knowledge and to accommodate an increasingly diverse group of users.

Copyright & plagiarism issues

An important issue that the present day library professionals are facing in providing electronic/digital information service is the large scale of piracy of software and plagiarism. The cost and timeliness in retrieving the information are also considered. When negotiating access with a publisher, the librarian must agree to certain restrictions on photocopying or distribution of electronic materials. Despite copyright notices and efforts to educate employees and users about intellectual property rights, electronic publications can be easily forwarded to people outside the licensed user group. The library is responsible for maintaining the awareness of all users about copyright issues.

Privacy/confidentiality

Maintaining privacy and confidentiality is another problem in accessing online information. To control pirating of software, copying or downloading all the contents of any e-resource at a time, right to obtain information and right to withhold or ban the access is essential and so there is a delicate challenge between privacy and rights to information. Now-a- days almost all the users are having their own e-mail accounts and they are often sending and receiving important information and even secret programmes and databases through e-mail itself and storing them for future usage. So maintaining privacy from e-mails is a great issue. Protecting one network from another to maintain confidentiality of information is another problem in securing databases on Internet and Intranet.

Online/Virtual Crimes and Security

"Privacy and security are two sides of the same coin," said Kurtz. "If we can improve Web security, we will be able to have a positive impact on privacy as well." Presently, Web/cyber crimes have become a common threat on internet. To overcome this issue, compulsory Virus Proof procedures should be adopted while downloading e-information from any other system. To secure the system from viruses, the databases can be modified by hacker proof procedures. Separate login and password systems are to be compulsorily adapted to the Network systems. In the LAN environment, the real danger is the gradual erosion of individual liberties through the automation, integration, and interconnection of many small, separate record keeping systems, each of which alone may seem innocuous, and wholly justifiable. To overcome the above database security problems and issues, it is essential to install a database security software or firewall technology like Norton Anti-virus software and IBM e-network Firewall technology to protect the databases.

Technology Challenges

Technology provides challenges to access information. The ALA's 1995 Code of Ethics clearly states that everyone should have access to information. The recent explosion of information available on the Internet presents challenges to the traditional American Library Association (ALA) code of ethics that is taught in library school. Librarians make ethical decisions every day on the basis of the culture of their organizations. Some organizations limit access to particular levels of employees by requiring a username and password; others may institute behind-the-scenes filtering software or restrictive policies for providing access to the entire Internet. Because these steps challenge the very essence of librarianship, the librarian must step in and voice concern for the patron's rights. Establishing well defined access policies will help to clarify who has access to the Internet, under what conditions, for what purposes, and with what restrictions. Policies should consider how to integrate the new technology and how its use reflects the objectives and values of the library.

Organizational Structure

Technology has broken down the rigid hierarchical structure of the organizations which is another important issue in changing the roles of the librarian in the knowledge society. Far from emulating the organization of conventional libraries, the organization and structure of digital libraries, and the division of labour within them, are open to considerable experimentation.

For example, as publishers and professional societies disseminate works electronically, they are testing how far their investments should incorporate the full range of library functions, and the digital libraries license content from publishers and professional societies that manage their own repositories.

Collection of e-resources

Collecting the materials and making it available to all current and future users is another core value of librarianship. The challenge is for the librarian to contribute to establish realistic collection-development policies covering acquisition of and provision of access to electronic resources for users now and in the future. With the increase in electronic resources, librarians and libraries are no longer just collecting and caring for print materials. Unlike a print book or a journal, electronic resources cannot be considered a permanent addition to a collection. Payment for a product covered by a license is a payment to use the information product for a period of time that is usually specified in a contract. This payment is not for the outright purchase of the product or for ownership of all the rights to that product. A digitized collection means that libraries share the use of the collections with other institutions, not only locally, but also globally. It is the publisher who dictates how much access will be provided, which issues will be available, and how much that access will cost.

CHANGING ROLES OF FUTURE ACADEMIC LIBRARY PROFESSIONAL

The changing role of library professional implies a set of updated skills needed for facing the challenges created by the latest web technologies in the e-learning environment. The emphasis will shift from technical skills in the library to communication, facilitation, training and management skills. Although technology presents the librarian with ethical challenges, the librarian is to be ready for the role of information professional in the connected networked world and they have to acquire skills that can be contributed to success in their new roles.

Leadership Role

One primary role of librarians is to provide leadership and expertise in the design, development, and ethical management of knowledge-based information systems in order to meet the information needs and obligations of the patron or academic institution. In the future, as now, we can expect the virtual library to be the organization that identifies, selects, negotiates for, and provides access to an incredible range of information resources on our behalf. At present, lot of virtual libraries have been created and managed by various institutions and organizations for e-learning and teaching professional. Hence library professional should enrich their management skills to play leadership role in the digital future, for organizing, managing and disseminating e-literacy to users.

Proactive Information Professional Role

The modern trend is for the role of the librarian to move from that of a passive intermediary role responsible for guiding patrons to appropriate information resources, towards that of a much more proactive professional role which includes analyzing and repackaging information, content information management systems and institute digital repository management systems.

ROLES OF INFORMATION SCIENTISTS IN DIGITAL LIBRARIES AND E-LITERACY

Librarians have to change their role in the e-learning environment by participating in e-learning experiments and becoming involved in universities' e-learning centers. They should invest in procuring e-learning tools and software and should develop their e-learning and ICT skills. Hans Roes addressed changes in education in general, and then focused on strategic opportunities in education for libraries. The opportunities for libraries, he mentioned, developing digital libraries as natural complements to digital learning environments to support educators with respect to the selection of adequate resources for a given course;

- Managing and indexing digital student portfolios and integrating them with other information resources offered by the library;

- Teaching information literacy to educate future knowledge workers, in traditional ways or via Internet-based instruction modules;
- Collaborating as part of multidisciplinary teams of experts to design courses;
- Providing a learning center to serve as a physical learning environment suitable for more active learning styles.

CONCLUSIONS

The remarkable growth of Internet has made significant revolution in all the areas of science and technology. Rather than using it as a tool for searching and retrieving information, Internet has become the king of all media, by which we can access virtual information and can build a virtual library to provide timely, quality service to the users. Librarians of this digital era are in the position to change their role as arbitrary information scientists/gatekeepers and to meet the challenges of the Internet, World Wide Web, on line access in the knowledge society. So they must enrich their knowledge with special skills of the latest IT developments, to browse, access and retrieve a particular information across the global networks and to organize and manage the information by building digital libraries and by which they can provide quality e-information service to the knowledge society. Library staff must be capable of working effectively in partnership with faculty members to enhance the strength of teaching and research. To be certain, there are many staff members of this kind in academic libraries today. In this as in other respects, part of the skills, library staff must develop is the ability to educate faculty members, helping them to understand the power and applicability of e-resources.

REFERENCES

- Abbott, Andrew. (1998). Professionalism and the Future of Librarianship. *Library Trends,* 46.3, 430-445.
- Dewey, Barbara. (2004). The Embedded Librarian: Strategic Campus Collaborations. *Resource Sharing & Information Networks* 17.(1/2), 5-17.
- Dugdale, Christine. (1999). The role of electronic reserves in serving and shaping new teaching and learning environments in UK universities. *Journal of Information Science.* 25(3), 183-192.
- Gamble, Lynne E. (1989). University Service: New Implications for Academic Librarians. *The Journal of Academic Librarianship* 14(6), 344-347.
- Janes, Joseph. (2001). *Digital Libraries as learning tools.* Tilburg: Ticer B.V., p.3.1.-3.6
- Joint, N. (2005). Strategic approaches to digital libraries and virtual learning environments (VLEs). *Library Review,* 54 (1), 5-9.
- Kasperek, Sheila, et al. (2006). Do a Little Dance: The Impact on Students when Librarians get involved in Extracurricular Activities. *The Journal of Academic Librarianship* 32(.6).
- Kinnie, Jim. (2002). Making a Case for the Tenure Banjo. *American Libraries* 33(10), 58.
- Lipka, Sara. (2004). The Secret Lives of Academics. *Chronicle of Higher Education* 51(8), 6.

10

IPR: National and International Provisions

Preeti Patel
Research scholar
Kishor John
Asst. Professor, OSD Higher Education,
Moti Tabela Indore (M.P.)

INTRODUCTION

Intellectual property laws and enforcement vary widely from jurisdiction to jurisdiction. Intellectual property laws confer a bundle of exclusive rights in relation to the particular form or manner in which ideas or information are expressed or manifested, and not in relation to the ideas or concepts themselves We live in a knowledge economy, where ideas generated by brilliant people and the inventions they make are the new currency. Intellectual property rights are legal rights, which result from intellectual activity in the industrial, scientific, literary and artistic fields. These rights give statutory expression to the moral and economic rights of creators in their creations. Intellectual property rights safeguard creators and other producers of intellectual goods and services by granting them certain time-limited rights to control the use made of those productions. These rights also promote creativity and the dissemination and application of its results and encourage fair-trading, which contributes to economic and social development. This article is a attempt to know the content and various aspects of IPRs in special reference to India and UNESCO.

INTERNATIONAL PROVISIONS FOR IPR MEASURES

The need for a system to protect IP internationally arose when foreign exhibitors refused to attend an International Exhibition of Inventions in Vienna in 1873 because they were afraid that their ideas would be stolen and exploited commercially in other countries. This led to the creation of the Paris Convention for the Protection of Industrial Property of 1883. The Paris Convention was the first major international treaty designed to help the people of one country obtain protection in other countries for their intellectual creations, in the form of industrial property rights. In 1886, copyright entered the international arena with the Berne Convention for the Protection of Literary and Artistic Works. In 1893, these two small bureaus united to form an international organization called the United International Bureaus for the Protection of Intellectual Property – best known by its French acronym, BIRPI. Based in Berne, Switzerland, with a staff of seven, BIRPI was the predecessor of what is today known as the World Intellectual Property Organization or WIPO (established on 1970). WIPO is a specialized agency of the UN, with a mandate to administer IP matters recognized by the UN Member States. There are about 21 international treaties in the field of intellectual property, which are administered by WIPO. The treaties fall into three groups namely treaties, which establish international protection; treaties, which facilitate international protection and treaties, which establish classification systems. India is also a member of the World Trade Organization (WTO established in 1995). The WTO agreement on Trade Related Aspects of

Intellectual Property (TRIPS) . This Agreement made protection of intellectual property an enforceable obligation of the Member States. TRIPS Agreement sets out minimum standards of intellectual property protection for Member States. A UN agency, namely, World Intellectual Property Organization (WIPO) based in Geneva administers treaties in the field of intellectual property. India is a member of WIPO. Department of Industrial Policy & Promotion is the nodal Department in the Government of India for all matters concerning WIPO.

CONTENTS COVERED IN IPRS

IPR connotes the right to literary, artistic and scientific work; performances of performing artists; phonographs and broad-cast; inventions in all fields of human endeavor; scientific discoveries; industrial designs; trademarks; service marks and commercial names and designations, and all other products resulting from intellectual activity in the industrial, scientific, literary and artistic fields. It is a generic term covering patents; registered design; trademark; copyright; layout of integrated circuits, trade secrets; geographical indicators and anti-competitive practices in contractual licenses.The term “Intellectual Property” denotes the specific legal rights –

1. Patents
2. Copy right
3. Designs
4. Trade Marks
5. Geographical indications

Apart of foresaid area IPR’s also dealt with in two more areas namely undisclosed information or Trade secrets and the Indian Contract act. Undisclosed information or Trade secrets as the name suggest is a secret known only to a few. The contract act does not deal with IPRs directly. It is a law dealing with contracts.

However IPRs are also subject to contracts and licenses. It is this sense that IPRs are governed by the Contract Act. These two areas along with the Copyright Act and Patents Act have bearing on computer software.

IPRS INITIATIVES IN INDIA IN SPECIAL REFERENCE TO DIGITAL ENVIRONMENT

Patents

A **Patent** is a legal monopoly, which is granted for a limited time by a country to the owner of an invention. Merely to have a patent does not give the owner the rights to use or exploit the patented invention. That right may still be affected by other laws such as health and safety regulation or the food and drugs regulation or even by other patents. The patent, in the eyes of the law, is a property right and it can be given away, inherited, sold, licensed and can even be abandoned. As it is conferred by the government, the government, in certain cases even after grant or even if it has been, in the meantime, sold or licensed, can revoke it. The Patents Act 1970, as amended by The Patents amendment) Act 2005. The Patents Rules, 2003, as amended by The (Amendment) Rules 2006.

- A Patent gives an inventor the right for a limited period to stop others from making, using, selling or importing an invention without the permission of the inventor. That is why patent is called a "negative right".
- Patents are generally concerned with functional and technical aspects of products and processes and must fulfill specific conditions to be granted.
- Most patents are for incremental improvements in known technology - evolution rather than revolution. The technology does not have to be complex.
- Patent rights are territorial; an Indian patent does not give rights outside of India.

- Patent rights last for up to 20 years in India and in most countries outside India.
- Depending on where you wish your patent to be in effect, you must apply to the appropriate body. In India, this is The Indian Patent Office. There are various Patent Offices around the world. Alternatively, a Patent Agent can apply on your behalf.

Copy Right

Copyright Registration in India gives the creators of a wide range of material, such as literature, art, music, sound recordings, films and broadcasts, economic rights enabling them to control use of their material in a number of ways, such as by making copies, issuing copies to the public, performing in public, broadcasting and use on-line. It also gives moral rights to be identified as the creator of certain kinds of material and to object to its distortion or its mutilation. (Material protected by copyright is termed a "work"). The purpose of copyright law in India is to allow copyright registrants to gain economic rewards for their efforts and so encourage future creativity and the development of new material which benefits us all. Copyright material is usually the result of creative skill and/or significant labour and/or investment and without protection; it would often be very easy for others to exploit material without paying the creator. Most uses of copyright material therefore require permission from the copyright owner. However there are exceptions to copyright, so that some minor uses may not result in copyright infringements. Copyright protection is automatic as soon as there is a record in any form of the material that has been created. Under the Indian Copyright Act there is a provision to register copyright although this is voluntary.

Designs

The Industrial Designs Bill, 1999 which replaces the Designs Act, 1911 on December 23, 1999 and is presently before the Lower House for its consideration.

Trademark

A Trademark is any sign which can distinguish the goods and services of one trader from those of another. A sign includes words, logos, colours, slogans, three-dimensional shapes and sometimes sounds and gestures. A trademark is therefore a "badge" of trade origin. It is used as a marketing tool so that customers can recognise the product of a particular trader. To be registrable in India it must also be capable of being represented graphically, that is, in words and/or pictures. A new Trademark regime has been introduced in India since September 15, 2003. The new Trade Marks Act, 1999 has many innovative features.

Service Marks

A mechanism is now available to protect marks used in the service industry. Thus businesses providing services like computer hardware and software assembly and maintenance, restaurant and hotel services, courier and transport, beauty and health care, advertising, publishing, educational and the like are now in a position to protect their names and marks.

Collective Marks

Marks being used by a group of companies can now be protected by the group collectively.

Well-known marks

Marks, which are deemed to be well known, are defined. Such marks will enjoy greater protection. Persons will not be able to register or use marks, which are imitations of well-known trademarks.

Enlarged scope of registration

Persons who get their marks registered for particular goods in a particular class and commence using their marks can sue and prevent other persons from

(i) Using the same or similar marks even for different goods falling in other classes;

(ii) Using the same or similar marks even only as part of their firm name or company name;

(iii) Using the same or similar mark only in advertising or on business papers;

(iv) Importing or exporting goods under the said trade mark;

(v) Unauthorized oral use of the said trademark.

Stringent punishment

Punishment for violating a trademark right has been enhanced. The offence has now been made cognizable and wide powers have been given to the police to seize infringing goods. At the same time the power of the Courts to grant expert injunctions have been amplified.

Appellate Board

An appellate board (IPAB) has been constituted based in Chennai for speedy disposal of Appeals and rectification applications.

Expedited procedure

Mechanisms have been set in place for expediting search and registration by paying five times the normal fee.

Enhanced renewal period

Registered trademarks need to be renewed every ten years.

GEOGRAPHICAL INDICATIONS

Geographical Indications of Goods are defined as that aspect of industrial property which refers to the geographical indication referring to a country or to a place situated therein as being the country or place of origin of that product. Typically, such a name conveys an assurance of quality and distinctiveness which is essentially attributable to the fact of its origin in that defined geographical locality, region or country. Under Articles 1 (2) and 10 of the Paris Convention for the Protection of Industrial Property, geographical indications are covered as an element of IPRs. They are also covered under Articles 22 to 24 of the Trade Related Aspects of Intellectual Property Rights (TRIPS) Agreement, which was part of the Agreements concluding the Uruguay Round of GATT negotiations.

India, as a member of the World Trade Organization (WTO), enacted the Geographical Indications of Goods (Registration & Protection) Act, 1999 has come into force with effect from 15th September 2003.

IPR IN DIGITAL CONTEXT

The issues mentioned above are specific to the library community. The libraries as a Service has allowed their users to read a document, to browse through the whole collection; to search through the library catalogue; to supply Xerox copy for specific individual research and education purpose; to procure photocopies of articles from other libraries or clearing centers; to widely distribute the re-produced copies of documents requiring public awareness and to provide inter library loan service. Whether all these activities will continue in the digital age? If digitization is considered as reproduction, it is clear that in digitization the initial work is merely changed into the digital form and the process of changing is accomplished by a machine, without any creativity. At the same time if it is considered as a translation from one language to another, the digitization is also a change from natural language of humans in to binary language of machine. In digitization however, there is no creativity involved and it could be considered as an activity similar to reprography. The copyright protects creative works. Simply transformation in to the digital form of an original document cannot be considered as creative. The transmission of information on Internet can be considered similar to broad casting and copyright law cannot be applied. Internet transmission is global in nature. A tangible object carrying a traditional work distributed lawfully comes under the principle of exhaustion of distribution right. It is not appropriate to apply this right to a work transmitted on Internet. The transmission on Internet is different from any tangible object fixing of the work.

Electronic publishing

Electronic publishing is an urgent aspect of current Information age. User's need fully changed in today ICT era, so the digital material is playing vital role in collection development of Library and Information Centers to satisfy day to day requirement of research scholars, faculty members, and students. Electronic Publishing covers all the aspect of as usual as print publishing. E- Publishing use email, internet, CD, DVDs, and on line resources for disseminate the information. Electronically published materials created and disseminate specifically for electronic publishing. PDF and similar formats are used in electronic publishing. Internet/Web and email) is electronic publishing. PDF and similar formats are also electronic publishing when the end-product (the PDF file) is intended primarily for on-screen viewing. Kist (1989) defined electronic publishing as "the application by publishers of a computer aided process, by which they find, capture, shape, store and update information content in order to disseminate it to a chosen audience" From Wikipedia, the free encyclopedia, electronic publishing includes the digital publication of e-books and electronic articles, and the development of digital libraries and catalogues.

IFLA's view on Copy right in Digital environment

1. IFLA maintains that unless libraries and citizens are granted exceptions which allow reasonable access and fair use for purposes which do not harm the interests of rights owners, and which are in the public interest and in line with fair practice such as education and research, there is a danger that only those who can afford information will be able to take advantage of the benefits of the Information Society.
2. In national copyright legislation, exceptions to copyright and related rights, allowed in the erne Convention and endorsed by the WIPO treaties, should be revised if necessary to ensure that permitted uses apply equally to information in electronic form and to information in print, and for copying over and above these provisions there should be administratively simple payment or licensing schemes.
3. Reformatting of material to make it accessible should not be considered an infringement of copyright and should be considered as reasonable access.
4. IFLA supports moves for differential and cheaper licensing tariffs for disadvantaged communities.
5. Temporary or technical copies which are incidental to the use of copyright material and which have no economic value should be excluded from the scope of the reproduction right
6. For works in digital format, without incurring a

further payment or seeking permission, all legitimate users of a library should be able to:

- Browse publicly available copyright material;
- Read, listen to, or view lawfully acquired publicly marketed copyright material privately, on site or remotely; (including material which has to be adapted for those with a learning disability or translated into a different language)
- Copy, or have copied for them by library and information staff a reasonable proportion of a digital work in copyright for personal, educational or research use.

7. IFLA believes that resource sharing plays a vital role in education, democracy, economic growth, health and welfare and personal development.
8. It facilitates access to a wider range of information, which would not otherwise be available to the user, library or country requesting it.
9. Resource sharing is not a mechanism to reduce costs but to expand availability to those who, for economic, technical or social reasons are unable to have access to the information directly. If a library has lawful access to a digital work, then providing access for any legitimate purpose such as research or study should be permitted under copyright law.
10. IFLA believes that Public lending is essential to culture and education. It should be available to all. Information packaged in all formats has and will become part of the lending stock. Lending in turn assists in the marketing of commercially packaged information and encourages sales.
11. IFLA believes that the lending of published materials by libraries should not be restricted by legislation and those contractual provisions.
12. Legislation should give libraries and archives

permission, where necessary, to convert copyright protected materials into digital format for preservation and conservation related purposes and libraries should be allowed to provide access to such materials as they would a book, including access both onsite and off-site.

13. National copyright legislation should render invalid any terms of a license that restrict or override exceptions or limitations embodied in copyright law where the license is established unilaterally by the rights owners without the opportunity for negotiation of the terms of the license by the user.
14. At a minimum the license should permit users to read, download, and print materials for their own personal purposes, without restrictions.

UNESCO guide lines for legal deposit and use of electronic publications 2

On the occasion of its meeting in Beijing in August 1996, the Conference of Directors of National Libraries (CDNL) requested UNESCO to publish this document for wide distribution in its Member States. The document, prepared by a CDNL Working Group chaired by Brian Lang, Chief Executive of the British Library, suggests guidelines for national libraries both in developing and developed countries on how to prepare proposals for the legal deposit of electronic publications and on how to house and maintain such publications. The main purposes of the UNESCO 'Guidelines for legal deposit legislation' are to develop a comprehensive collection of national publications and to compile an authoritative national bibliographic record, in order to ensure their preservation and provide easy access to them. It is just as appropriate that these two essential functions should apply to the electronic publishing environment as they do to the traditional print on paper environment. It was also published on paper in the working series of the General Information Program and UNISIST.

HOW DO IPR AFFECT ACCESS TO INFORMATION?

When a customer purchases a book in a bookstore neither the owner of the bookshop, nor the owner of copyright in the book, will be able to know, or control, how or where the consumer uses that book. IPR fundamentally change that dynamic by forcing an ongoing relationship between the copyright owner and the user, and enable the copyright owner to limit such access and use to a single computer, or to certain technologies or time periods, and to automatically prohibit uses that are not permitted by the copyright owners' license. Access to works is locked up, and individuals only have the rights that owners provide for them or license them with, which could be far less than allowed in the Copyright law.

Anti-circumvention measures provided in the Intellectual Property Chapter of the U.S. Free Trade Agreement far exceed countries' international obligations. These Copyright protection measures ban acts of circumvention, and the distribution of tools and technologies used for circumvention. They ban circumvention of technologically-protected material, thus preventing students and educators from accessing material they have purchased to make excerpts for use in lessons. Local technology vendors would be banned from producing or selling technologies or devices that educators need if they are to use copyright exceptions that would otherwise apply to protected digital material that they have purchased.

IPR MORE EFFECTIVELY WORK WITH DIGITAL RESOURCE MANAGEMENT

DRMs pose a serious threat to the ability of the public to access and use works in the public domain. They have the potential to protect works indefinitely. This permanent lock-up of public domain material runs contrary to the principle of balance in copyright law. They also threaten to lock up and permanently render works inaccessible because data stored in proprietary DRM formats (whether it be songs, software, e-books or other data) is at a much greater risk of being lost once the playback media becomes obsolete. Due to the lack of inter-operability in DRM-related services, there is the potential that large collections of content will not be able to be accessed at all (Cameron, 2007, p. 7). This has a serious effect on the availability and accessibility of information and shrinks what is available via the public domain. Consider the serious implications this will have for legal deposit libraries and archives, in particular. While DRMs can certainly prevent illegal copying, and public distribution, of copyrighted works, the capabilities of these systems are far wider. They can as easily prevent copying and distribution of public domain works, as well as copyrighted ones. Furthermore, even though copyright law confers on copyright owners, the right to control only *public* performances and displays of their works, DRMs can also be used to control *private* performances and displays of digital content DRMs prevent the exercise of fair use/fair dealing rights and other copyright privileges. Furthermore, they can be used to compel users to view content they would prefer to avoid, for example, they can prevent fast-forwarding on DVDs. This exceeds the bounds of copyright These technological protection measures could have far-reaching implications for broadcast technologies (such as digital television and radio) and could restrict private, non-commercial uses of broadcasting content. They could be used by rights-holder, to restrict access to information that is in the public domain, not copyrightable, or has been permissively licensed. They could also be detrimental for innovation and competition policy.

There are many different types of DRMs which helps

to applying IPR in digital environment, some more restrictive than others. The following are some examples which can have an impact on access to information or affect librarians and archivists from carrying out their daily functions:

(i) Limiting a document to one PC or one user

(ii) Specifying the number of times a document can be opened

(iii) Limit document lifetime (minutes, days, months)

(iv) Enable or disable printing

(v) Define number of printed copies allowed

(vi) Enable or disable copy/pasting facilities

(vii) Enable or disable saving to file

(viii) Protection against file copying.

(ix) Encryption facilities obscure or scramble information and need a decryption key to decipher the material;

(xi) When printing an article from the Internet, sometimes only the first and last pages print out or they print out in garbled script.

(xii) DRMs also prohibit the use of generics, for example, Samsung printers will not work without an original Samsung cartridge.

PRIVACY ISSUES WITH IPR

1. Login and registration facilities enable the rights holder to establish who is the user and only allows registered users further access to the content;
2. Use biometric identification, such as iris scans, fingerprints and facial recognition;
3. Some DRMs, like spyware, attempt to send information back to the publisher or other parties, about the user, without the end user's knowledge and approval;

4. Investigation functionality allows copyright owners to gather and analyses detailed information about users' reading, viewing and listening habits. These activities are ones that are typically performed in the privacy of one's home, where they would have no expectation of being watched;
5. Work to control access and use of content. They can control whether the content may be reproduced, including the number of copies that may be printed online, the length of time for which the content may be accessed, and whether or not it may be cut and pasted. National archives and legal deposit libraries,
6. Legal deposit libraries and archives should be empowered to take such steps as an initial conservation measure, when such materials are received or at any point thereafter.
7. It is very difficult to determine Libraries should therefore insist, as a matter of course, that rights-owners provide adequate information about IPR on their e-products, using information labels, instruction manuals, explanatory leaflets and discs. When purchasing access to electronic resources,
8. Librarians should negotiate licenses, which do not override fair use/fair dealing provisions or any copyright exceptions, or which do not restrict or prohibit access to the product or content. Libraries should refuse to accept products which have DRMs that interfere with or prevent rightful access for which they have paid. They should demand refunds on products which are marketed to libraries but which are in accessible to their users.

CHALLENGES OF IPR

When a customer purchases a book in a bookstore neither the owner of the bookshop, nor the owner of copyright in the book, will be able to know, or control, how or where the consumer uses that book. IPR fundamentally change that dynamic by forcing an ongoing relationship between the copyright owner and the user, and enable the copyright owner to limit such access and use to a single computer, or to certain technologies or time periods, and to automatically prohibit uses that are not permitted by the copyright owners' license. Access to works is locked up, and individuals only have the rights that owners provide for them or license them with, which could be far less than allowed in the Copyright law.

Anti-circumvention measures provided in the Intellectual Property Chapter of the U.S. Free Trade Agreement far exceed countries' international obligations. These Copyright protection measures ban acts of circumvention, and the distribution of tools and technologies used for circumvention. They ban circumvention of technologically-protected material, thus preventing students and educators from accessing material they have purchased to make excerpts for use in lessons. Local technology vendors would be banned from producing or selling technologies or devices that educators need if they are to use copyright exceptions that would otherwise apply to protected digital material that they have purchased. "Digital technology enables [publishers] to track and charge for every instance of electronic access, even for browsing. The resulting market power then allows the publisher to impose monopoly prices and potentially oppressive terms on users, including libraries, academies, institutes and research centers, and to ignore the social consequences that ensue from the inability of research organizations to pay for such access." Most copying of print-based material in libraries is for educational, research or private study purposes or for preservation. The reasons usually given for copying are because users are unable to read the material in the library (material is in demand or reference only) or because the user wishes to read it at a more convenient time (time shifting). Despite rights owner concerns about loss of sales there is no evidence that copying *reasonable amounts* from copyright protected works displaces sales. Those who copy would not necessarily buy a work if prevented from copying it. There is no reason to believe that this pattern will not also be true of copying from digital works. *"Librarians and information professionals recognize, and are committed to support the needs of their patrons to gain access to copyright works and the information and ideas they contain. They also respect the needs of authors and copyright owners to obtain a fair economic return on their intellectual property. Effective access is essentialin achieving copyright's objectives. IFLA supports balanced copyright law that promotes the advancement of society as a whole by giving strong and effective protection for the interests of rights holders as well as reasonable access in order to encourage creativity, innovation, research, education and learning.*

LIBRARIES AND IPR

Libraries are the repositories of human knowledge; they store our past, our present and our future and provide it on the demand of user. In current information communication technology age libraries convert them in to digital form. The electronic libraries acquire store and disseminate data/ information in electronic form. Libraries have adopted internal regulations, abide by national laws and international practices with the aim to achieve their goals, i.e. satisfy people's quest for knowledge and creative works. While almost all libraries and librarians acknowledge the need to abide by Intellectual Property law that protects the interests of authors and creators, initial and subsequent right-holders, they do also show unwillingness to transform from organizations that enable access to knowledge into gatekeepers of locked-in, inaccessible knowledge. Digital library as repositories of works include in their contents copyrighted works as well as works under no copyright such as works in the public domain. Digital library could include in their contents works delivered in any medium and format. Frequently, Digital library are the licensed creators of derivative works, i.e. a variety of digital media and formats of the same work furnished to it. A Digital library, also, could contain many different copyrights. For example a textual article or e-book is protected as literary works, photographs as artistic works, a music DVD or CD as a musical work. The Digital library's website could also subject to different copyrights. Components could be protected by the right of communication to the public or qualify for the database right protection. The Copyright issues that pertain to the legitimate operation of a Digital library are complex and usually difficult to resolve once a dispute arose. Intellectual Property has always been in the crossroads of conflicting interests among the creators, right-holders, and the general public, and it has always been a vexing problem to balance among conflicting copyright-related interests. To manage the distribution of complete publications or individual content elements, two licensing metaphors are implemented.

1. A Master Agreement broadly defines the rules and conditions that apply to all licensing agreements negotiated between the purveyor and a content provider; only one Master Agreement may be defined between the provider and the purveyor. In practice, RMS assumes that the purveyor will enter into one or more collection agreements with each of its content suppliers. At the time the first license agreement is executed between the two parties, a Master Agreement is created along with one or more Collection Agreements (see below) in the purveyor's RMS database.
2. Collection Agreements are used to specify the rules and conditions that apply to specific sets of materials licensed by a content provider to the purveyor. This

agreement takes the form of a list of publications and the associated terms and conditions under which these publications may be issued to end-users (one or more Collection Agreements may be defined and simultaneously managed between the purveyor and a customer).

CONCLUSION

In this changing scenario, the librarian is going to be a highly skilled professional whose total commitment would be as navigators to global intellectual resources as facilitators, instructors, gatekeepers of knowledge interpreters, evaluators, consultants, researchers, information managers, promoters and has improved the image of the librarians by playing all the roles successfully. The fair use of print material by allowing use of reprography techniques in a sensible way for research study and educational purpose is understood. But in the context of electronic information, because it is disseminated to a larger population, it is difficult to evaluate, realize "reasonable use", access and control the encroachment of copyright law. To follow the IPRs in library and information centers it is necessary to that our Information professional also know about IPRs guide lines for fair use. The Librarians should continue to work as channel for the free flow of information between the owners of information and the users of the information. IFLA, UNESCO or any Government does not want to see an environment where total control over access to information is in the hands of a small number of large transnational companies. If all uses of information are controlled, only the affluent will be able to receive the benefit of access to the world's creative output. These organizations are concerned that, unless this control is limited, it will interfere with the greater good of society. One cannot rely on rights owners to put the interests of society first. That is the role of governments. Although no one denies rights owners the right to obtain a return on their investment, limitations in the form of exceptions must be part of the equation to ensure that society may also obtain a similar return on its investment in education and research. Only in this way will a balance be achieved.

REFERENCE

- National seminar on information policies and cyber laws. 4-6 December 2000.
- Bangalore. Sarada Rang Nathan Endowment for Library Science. Bangalore, 2000.
- Panda, K.C. and others. Copyright law in the electronic age. In Access to electronic information: Papers presented at the SIS-97, - 16th Annual Convention and Conference. 29-31, January, 1997. Bhubaneswar ed. By M.Mahapatra and others.Society for Information Science, Bhubaneswar Chapter, Bhubaneswar, 1997. pp
- Lakshmana Moorthy, A. and Karisiddappa, C.R. Copyright and electronic information,
- ibid—pp 403-416
- Bomanwar, V.J.Intellectual property rights and new information society. In Towards the new information society of tomorrow: Innovations, challenges and impact. Papers presented at the 49th FID conference and congress, New Delhi, 11-17 October 1998. ed by N.M.Malwad and others. FID publications No.719. INSDOC, New Delhi, 1998. Ibid pp iv-31-33.
- Murthy, T.A.V. and Jain, S.P. Network access to electronic documents and its copyright implications to developing countries. Ibid. pp iv 40-44.
- Deming Zhou, Chinese copyright protection system and the challenges of digital technology. Ibid pp iv – 45-50.
- Lakshmana Moorthy, A. and Karisiddappa, C.R. Intellectual property rights and virtual libraries. Ibid – pp iv 51-61.
- Tushar Kanti Shah. Science and friction in the field of intellectual property rights.
- Ibid-pp iv 62-70. (20 refs)

- Lakshmana Moorthy, A. and Karisiddappa, C.R. Electronic publishing: Impact and implications on library and information centers In Digital libraries. Dynamic store house of digitized information. Papers presented at the SIS 96 – 15th Annual Convention and Conference. 18-20 Janaury 1996, Bangalore. ed. By N.M.Malwad and others. New Age International Publishers, New Delhi, 1996. pp15-35.
- World Intellectual Property Organization. *Treaty on the Protection of Broadcasting Organizations.* Retrieved 31 August 2008 from http://www.wipo.int/edocs/mdocs/copyright/en/sccr_11/sccr_11_3.pdf
- International Federation of Libraries and Institutions (IFLA). Committee on Copyright and Other Legal Matters (CLM). 2002. IFLA's Position Paper on Copyright in the Digital Environment. Retrieved 7 September 2008 from http://www.ifla.org/III/clm/p1/pos-dig.htm
- International Federation of Library Associations and Institutions, Library Copyright Alliance and Electronic Information for Libraries. Provisional Committee on Proposals Related to the 16. International Intellectual Property Alliance. June 15, 2005. Comments on Theme Four. What is the impact of copyright law, both at international and national levels, on education and research. Retrieved 31 August 2008 from http://www.wipo.int/roller/comments/ipisforum/Weblog/theme_four_what_is_the
- Commission on Intellectual Property Rights. 2002a. *Integrating Intellectual Property Rights and Development Policy. Report of the Commission on Intellectual Property Rights.* London, United Kingdom. Retrieved on 18 October 2008 from http://www.iprcommission.org/papers/text/final_report/reporthtmfinal.htm
- Commission on Intellectual Property Rights. 2002b. *Press Release: Independent Commission Finds Intellectual Property Rights Impose Costs on Most Developing Countries and Do Not Help to Reduce Poverty.* September 12, 2002, London. United Kingdom. Retrieved 31 August 2008. from http://www.biotech-info.net/independent_commission.html
- Kallinikou, D. (2008) Archives, Libraries and Copyright. *Proceedings of the conference, Archives, Libraries and the Law in the era of Information Society, Athens, February 2-3, 2006,* http://www.nipo.in/ accessed on 23-09.2011

- Pedley, P. (2007), *Digital Copyright*, Facet
- Tareq M. Alrashid...etal (1998). Safeguarding Copyrighted Contents Digital Libraries and Intellectual Property Management-lib magazine. Available at http://www.dlib.org/dlib/april98/04barker.html accessed on 25.07.13
- http://crl.du.ac.in/ical09/papers/index_files/ical-117_142_311_2_RV.pdf accessed on 28- 09- 2011
- http://desktoppub.about.com/od/glossary/g/Electronic-Publishing.htm accessed on 28- 09- 2011
- http://www.unesco.org/webworld/memory/legaldep.htm accessed on 28- 09- 201

11

Library Software: Criteria for Selection

Ashish Kumar Sharma
Assistant Librarian, Central library,
Gurukul Kangri University Haridwar (U.K.) India

ABSTRACT

In the process of automation libraries and information centres the acquisition of software package is an important stage. Software in general, is a set of programs and accompanying documentation that direct computers to perform desired functions. In simple terms, "a software program is a set of instructions for a computer. In other words, it refers to all programs that are written to be executed on a computer. The programs are written in number of different languages called programming language. Evaluation of software is the process of examing in details the various features and performance in view of the defined guidelines of user requirement. The purpose of evaluation is to diagnose the missing features, while selecting any software package depending upon particular application. In this paper, an attempt has been made to cover the various aspect of library software. Vary briefly, the definition, types and criteria for selection library automation software, functions and popular library software have been covered.

Keywords: Library Automation, Types of Software, Library Software, Information and Communication Technology.

INTRODUCTION

Application of Information and Communication Technology (ICT) in library during the past few decades have brought effective changes in the way gathering information and its organization in libraries. Dissemination process is also influenced by the ICT application. This is an era of information revolution. Scientific, technical and other literature both in paper and in electronic form has been increasing exponentially beyond imagination. Information technology could provide a quantum jump in speedy accessibility, use, generation and communication of information. The developments in information technology and its application in library and information service sector has effected drastic changes in the way information is collected, stored, retrieved and disseminated for the benefit of actual and potential users of library system. Libraries and information centres are engaged in reassessing their source and services on the one hand and add new sources and systems like CD-ROM, multimedia, etc., on meet the changing needs with improved services.

The sources of library automation mostly depend upon the nature of the software used for the purpose. The hardware requirements usually follow the choice of the software. But in most of our libraries the opposite trends is seen. The hardware is purchased first as and when the funds are available and then the software is chosen with lot of considerations. This makes the implementation of the automation activities difficult. The ideal situation is to approved by the authority and then purpose the hardware according to the requirements. Since the real benefits from computerization comes from the appropriate software, rather than hardware alone, choice of the software is utmost importance that needs proper planning and consideration.

DEFINITION

Software is a package of a collection programmes. Each programme consists of a step by step instruction to attend a particular task. Evaluation of software is the process of examining in detail the various features and their performance in view of the defined guidelines of user requirement. The purpose of evaluation is to diagnose the missing features, while selecting any software package depending upon particular application say for example "Library automation".

The wrong choice of library software will have a deleterious impact on budgets, efficiency, motivation and ultimate usage. Therefore, one should thoroughly evaluate the software packages both from the view point of its functionality and the usability through some procedures

A software library is a suite of data and programming code that is used to develop software programs and applications. It is designed to assist both the programmer and the programming language compiler in building and executing software[1].

Software means *computer instructions or data.* Anything that can be stored electronically is software[2]

SOFTWARE CATEGORIES

Software, in common, is a set of programs and accompanying documentation that direct computers to perform desired functions. In simple terms, a software program is a set of instructions for a computer. In other words, it refers to all programs that are written to be executed on a computer. There are four basic types of software. These are[3]:

- System software (also known as the operating system) is a collection of programs that manages all the concurrent tasks being performed by a computer, including the execution of application software programs.

- Utility software is a set of programs that performs routine day-to-day tasks, such as listing or compressing data, copying files, etc.
- Application software performs specialized functions like library automation and the MIS functions mentioned in an organization, or other useful work not related directly to the operation of the computer itself.
- Package is computer application consisting of one or more programs created to perform a particular type of work.

SYSTEM SOFTWARE

System software is a set of one or more programs, deigned to control the operation of a computer. System software makes the operation of the computer system more effective and efficient. In general, system software supports the following:

- Smooth running of the other software.
- Communicate with peripheral devices.
- Support the development of other types of software.
- Monitor the use of various hardware resources.

UTILITY SOFTWARE

It is a set of programs that perform routine day-to-day tasks, such as listing or compressing data, copying files, printing, storing etc. this is also called system support program/software. The utility software is so designed it can perform maintenance work on the system or its components. Therefore, it is also known as Service Software. Examples of utility software's are PC Tools, Norton Utility etc.

APPLICATION SOFTWARE

Application software performs specialized functions or rather useful work not related directly to the operation of the computer itself. Examples are LIBSYS, Soul (specific purpose).

SOFTWARE PACKAGE

Software Package is computer application consisting of one or more programs created to perform a particular type of work. It is designed to satisfy the needs of many organizations. Examples are Lotus 123, Excel, Ventura, Page Maker, MS-Word, CorelDraw, PowerPoint etc.

PROCEDURE/CRITERIA FOR SELECTION LIBRARY AUTOMATION SOFTWARE

The following procedures/criteria may be considered to evaluate software packages and their features. As a first step one has to carefully examine the existing documentation in relation to the package and also collect information from various sources about the reputation of the software developers.

- An integrated software package.
- Compatible to various hardware systems.
- Operation in a multi-user environment.
- Operation in a networked environment.
- User friendly and menu driven.
- Least response time.
- Capable of handling bibliographical, numerical as well as textual data, also variable field, sub-fields and repeatable fields lengths.
- Support data security through passwords.
- Provision data security through passwords.
- Provision for thesaurus and authority file maintenance.
- Output facility through card printing, bibliographies and on magnetic media.
- Facilitate search through Boolean logic, single term

search and subsequent coordination, multiple term search, parenthetical grouping (=, >, <) set building, truncation (left, right, in between), adjacency search, wild card, field directed searching.

- Import export of data through standard exchange format.
- Provide powerful scanner capabilities.
- Display, sort and print records as per user defined formats.
- Software support by well written manuals (user/ programmers/system manger level), online helps, tutorials etc.
- www Interfacing.
- Multi-media compatibility.

In the world of fast changing IT, the above criteria cannot be definitive of all times but will have to be subjected to regular review to accommodate newer and fast changing LIS environment requirements.

FUNCTION OF LIBRARY AUTOMATION SOFTWARE PACKAGES

The objective of any library software package is to mechanize all the activities of the library. It makes easy, mainly the repetitive and tedious jobs of the library. Library software package also saves considerable time of the librarian and makes him more responsible to his duties. The major functions of the library software package can be divided according to the area/section/ department of the libraries where computerization is required. The major area/ sections are:

- Acquisition related functions
- Cataloguing
- Circulation control
- Serials control
- Reference and Information retrieval

- Administration, accounting and financial control.

Besides the major area as mentioned above, the library software package is expected to perform in other specific areas such as:

Information regarding present status or past history of a document in the library (i.e, book, periodical or any other material).

- Abstracting functions
- Indexing functions.
- Personalised information services i.e. SDI.
- Union catalogue related functions.
- OPAC searching.
- Database related functions.
- User profiles, mailing list, and other user-related functions.
- Statistics and reporting.
- Stock verification related functions.
- Exporting and importing of data.
- Barcode generation.
- Access and searching of Internet.
- Multimedia capabilities.
- Online acquisition, storage and retrieval capabilities.
- Access to electronic information.
- Providing safety and security to the vital information.

The above list is only an illustrative one, depending upon the type of library and there services.

POPULAR LIBRARY AUTOMATION SOFTWARE IN INDIA

A list of some popular library automation software is given below:

- **CDS/ISIS (DOS), WINSIS (GUI)** design and develop by UNESCO, in India NISSAT/ DSIR

Special feature **:** Although not a true library automation software package, it helps to develop automation Software package based on it. It consists of a set of computer programs that perform a variety of functions related to information storage and retrieval.

- **LIBMAN** design and develop by Datapro consultancy services, Pune

  Special feature **:** A versatile, user friendly package designed for small and medium libraries. It has a two level access to library automation - a restricted one for members and an unrestricted one for the librarians.

- **LIBSYS** design and develop by Libsys Corporation, New Delhi.

  Special feature **:** It is most comprehensive and popular library software package available in India. It is a fully integrated multi-user system operation on UNIX/VMS/LAN platforms and supports all activities relating to computerization of library operations.

- **SANJAY** design and develop by DESIDOC, Matcalf House, New Delhi.

  Special feature **:** A library automation package based on CDS/ISIS is capable of interlinking two or more databases for a single application, handling numerical calculations and carrying out library housekeeping operations.

- **SOUL** design and develop by INFLIBNET Centre Ahamedabad.

  Special feature **:** A Windows based library management software package covering all aspects of library automation meant for university libraries. It is a user friendly software designed by using client-server Architecture which imparts extra strengths to storage capacity, multiple access to single database, various level of security, back-up and storage facilities etc. The software is designed and developed exclusively to work under university environment. It is available at nominal cost. It is meant for all types of libraries.

- **SLIM** ++ design and develop by Algorthyms Company, Pune.

  Special feature **:** A complete library automation package, same version can be used as both standalone and network environment. It is meant for all types of libraries.

- **Alice for windows, OASIS for DOS,** design and develop by Soft Link Pvt., Australia and Marketed in India by Soft Link Asia, New Delhi.

  Special feature **:** A comprehensive library automation software package having an integrated library and information management system brings powerful automatic document and resources control within the reach of all organizations. Modules are grouped into one of the three sets- standard modules, advanced modules and special modules.

- **GRANTHALAYA** design and develop by NISCAIR, New Delhi.

CONCLUSION

Selection and evaluation of software package for library system is not an easy task for many reasons. Local availability and low price should not be the criteria for the selection of software package for the library whose functions and services are globalizing. Therefore the selected software should support not only automate the traditional library services but also contribute and avail the resources and services of the virtual library system to satisfy the dynamic needs of its users. A large number of library software packages are available in India and are yet to prove their usefulness in libraries. Library automation has become a necessity now, if the library has to survive in the present day electronic environment. For that purpose one should be caution and judicious in the selection and evaluations of the software package for the library.

REFERENCE

- http://www.techopedia.com/definition/3828/software-library
- http://www.webopedia.com/TERM/S/software.html
- Sandha, D.P. (2004). Software Component In M. Mahapatra and D.B.Ramesh (Ed) information technology applications in libraries a text book for beginners, Reproprint: Bhubaneshwar 62.
- Scamnell, Alison (1997), Hand Book of Special Librarianship and Information Work, Aslib London.
- Mishra,R.K.(1999). Library Software Selection: An Analysis IASLIC Bulletin. 44(3), 125-132.
- Morris Anne and Dyer, Hilary. (1998). Human Aspects of Library Automation.
- Li, L. L. (2009). Emerging Technologies for Academic Librarians in the Digital Age. London: Chandos Publishing.
- Rowley, G. E. (1998). The basic of Information Technology. London: Bingley.

12

Digital Era Librarians: Leadership Qualities

Sunil Kumar Tiwari

Guest Lecturer, LIS, Govt TRS College, Rewa (M.P.)

ABSTRACT

Leadership is an important issue in all sectors wherever there is a team working together to achieve a common goal. Library is also an organization where a team of professional, semi-professional and non-professional employees strive to serve a common purpose, namely, to cater to their clientele in the best possible way. So, the leadership issue continues to hold an important niche in the management thoughts related with librarianship. With the passing of decades and centuries many things changed shapes in the arena of the Librarianship. The shift from micro to macro information, the changes in format of resources, the entrance of upcoming technologies to cause radical shift in dimensions of information storage and retrieval; and many other factors have contributed to the growth of Digital Era Librarianship. There seem to be a need of thinking proactively about the ways to combat this challenge.

This paper seeks to capture the ways of traditional leadership in our field. It also attempts to cover the new challenges that are cropping up in the recent years. Ultimately it endeavors to seek out the leadership ways that helps them to suit the need of digital librarianship.

The role of traditional librarians has been explored in details. Different factors responsible for the enactment of that role have been dissected. Those found lacking have been adjusted against the ones that are seemingly most effective to suit today's LIS leadership scenario. It was premised that not only the copybook leadership principles, but other heuristics also go a long way to make a good leader for the digital era librarianship. Techno-savvy, skilled leaders with an aptitude of timely psycho-social interpretation of the intricacies of the challenges of the modern day librarianship are required. Only this dedicated team leaders can motivate and lead a complex band of LIS professionals.

All the aspects of digital era leadership for LIS domain came under the microscope here. The paper thus tries to present a framework to achieve better our goal and mission i.e. the ultimate usercentred LIS universe under the dynamic leadership of the digital librarian.

Keywords : Librarianship, Digital era, Leadership Skills, LIS Leaders, Libraries & Information Centers

INTRODUCTION

Leadership is an important issue in all sectors wherever there is a team working together to achieve a common goal. Library is also an organization where a team of professional, semi-professional and non-professional employees strive to serve a common purpose, namely, to cater to their clientele in the best possible way. So, the leadership issue continues to hold an important niche in the management thoughts related with librarianship. With the passing of decades and centuries many things changed shapes in the arena of the Librarianship. The shift from micro to macro information, the changes in format of resources, the entrance of upcoming technologies to cause radical shift in dimensions of information storage and retrieval; and many other factors have contributed to the growth of Digital Era Librarianship. There seem to be a need of thinking proactively about the ways to combat this challenge. The Main objectives of this study are given below :

- To analyze and explore the changing vision and the roles of leadership qualities for library professionals so as to meet the changes and challenges of the digital era.
- To trace an outline of the evolution in the role of librarianship.
- To discuss about the various skills needed for the library professionals to meet the present online and digital needs of the user.

IN THE TRADITIONAL LIBRARIES

In the initial days, books were few and far between; copied by scribes, almost always backed by the royal patronage. Users were the royalty and the topmost rung of the social Manpower Management and Developmentlayers; whereas a few very scholarly people, favoured by the affluent class might have allowed sniffing perfumes of the knowledge fragrance.

With printing, there came a fresh bridge of hope in the knowledge field with books printed in multiplied numbers and more and more people came into contact of books.

Gradually the Public Library Movement in different countries brought in the concept of 'People's University' and the commoners were included in the priviledges of enjoyment of knowledge embodied in books.

ROLE IN THE TRADITIONAL LIBRARIANSHIP

With the flourishing of the libraries as a centre of knowledge, it became evident that a librarian and his team were needed for preserving the books and later the periodicals. The establishment had become vast and the basic service of preserving books along with occasional readership had multiplied into acquisition, processing, storage, dissemination, preservation and conservation. Gradually all of those blossomed into intricate branches with many library scientists offering theoretical and practical treatises on different aspects of librarianship. All of that literature was of the same opinion on one count: all were preaching custodianship.

IN THE NEW AGE LIBRARIES

The new age librarianship brought out several changes, the most important being the shift from possession cum custodianship to access. There were several dramatic changes in the realm of LIS. The formats were diversified from print to digital via other non-print mediums. Some such changes are listed below :

- From possession to access
- From custodianship to facilitator
- From guardian to friend (of users)
- From reader to user
- From time-bound access to any-time-access
- From space-bound access to anywhere-access
- From librarian (or library-centred) to user-centred
- From rigidity to flexibility
- From ascetic environment to informal environment
- From specified/strict norms to Information Commons
- From strict disciplined library to relaxed pursuit of knowledge
- From one format to diversified formats
- From direction (from library staff) to participation (in the decisions)

FROM COPYBOOK LEADERSHIP TO HEURISTICS

Leadership is a quality to lead a team of workers. This is one of the most important qualities in the managerial capabilities. As is always said the strength of a chain is in the point of its weakest link, the librarian as a team-leader has always the role of motivator in such a way that all his team members become capable to work (at least) adequately as per the requirements of the job in hand. In the traditional era, all the roles of staff employed at Challenges in Library Management System (CLMS 2012) different sections were well defined. The main consideration was monitoring the routine work and to supervise the exigencies. In the digital era- as we have seen above- many changes occurred to change this status quo. In fact, it is a time for constant change. In this transition period for being a dynamic leader, the librarian needs to consider several aspects:

- Leading from the front
- Practice before preaching
- Better among equals
- Friendly- not bossy- attitude
- The depth of subject knowledge in the area of the job-at hand
- Awareness of the personal as well as social limitations of the staff (as well as himself)
- Assigning right person to right work
- Understanding the special aptitudes of staff
- Keeping in mind likings and disliking of staff while allocating jobs
- Remembering the invisible presence of the users while designing services and passing this attitude to co-staff
- Instituting proper orientation training for the new recruits
- Organizing regular refresher courses for the staff
- Regular ICT Workshops for staff
- Giving extra priviledges to staff as a reward and recognition of good work
- Arranging invited lectures by eminent Library &

Information professionals

- Allocating suitable infrastructure for every service points
- Providing ergonomic as well as aesthetic furniture for the staff

FROM CUSTODIAN TO FACILITATOR

Librarianship has traversed a long journey and we have to weed out some of our older concepts while adopting quite a few new ones to suit our changing needs. The role of library leaders are now to nurture a breed of techno savvy, skilled manpower equipped to serve a new brand of techno-savvy users. Users of digital era know a lot of things beforehand. So the library team has to go a step forward and to be aware of the quality resources available in the digital (as well as print) scenario.

DIGITAL ERA CHALLENGES

Due to its radically different nature from the traditional era, digital era provides multifarious benefits but it also offers manifold challenges. So the leadership in today's environment needs many skills and competencies in today's multi-user, multitasking online learning environment.They should have adequate technical knowledge of Operating System Software, Word Processing Software, Power Point Presentation Software, Spreadsheet, Graphics, Database Management Systems, Webpage Development and ContentManagement Software, CD ROM Database Searching, Networking Concepts, Digital Library Management Software, etc. Free and Open Source Software are to be used as much as possible. They should have a thorough understanding of knowledge resources (both in traditional and digital form), very adoptive towards change, pro-active, strategy-planner, flexible.

KNOWLEDGE ECONOMY TOWARDS

Physical as well as virtual space has now been utilised for library/information activities. In this changed and challenged environment, copybook leadership is no help. So, a library leader in the digital era has to be innovative, enthusiastic, and pro-active.With clarity of vision and the judicious use of the web 2.0 tools as well as heuristic knowledge, his mission is to create a user-centred library. The journey towards 'Knowledge Economy' will only be fulfilled if all stakeholders in the knowledge chain (from inception to dissemination to feedback to further creation of new/modified knowledge) take active and interactive participation in the whole process.

CONCLUSION

Whatever changes and challenges happened over the time, Creth (1996) has said that the "values that are the foundation of the library profession should remain the same into the next century...values of service, quality, universal access, and co-operation".

REFERENCES

- Creth, S. D. (1996) The Electronic Library: Slouching Toward the Future or Creating a New Information Environment Follett Lecture Series. Available from: http://www.ukoln.ac.uk/services/papers/follett/creth/ paper.html (retrieved on: 12/01/2012)
- Marchionin, Gary and Maurer, Hermann (1995). The role of Digital Library in teaching and learning.Communication of the ACM, 38(4).
- Thamaraiselvi, G. Vision and the Changing Roles of the Future cademic Library Professional in the ELearning Environment. Avlavil at : http://crl.du.ac.in/ical09/papers/index_files/ical-23_154_338_1_RV.pdf (retrieved\ on 20/01/2012)

13

Current Trends in Curriculum Reforms in LIS Education in India

Surbhi Saini

UGC-NET, Research and Teaching Assistant (RTA), Dept. of Lib. & Inf. Sci., School of Social Sciences (SOSS), Indira Gandhi NationalOpen University (IGNOU), Maidan Garhi, New Delhi-110068, India

ABSTRACT

S.R. Ranganathan gives the new subject to the tree of Universe of knowledge as like a new sweet fruit. The new branch of the tree gives the new hope for the students. Things never generate in the day, it is a fruit of hard work of several night and days. But time to time the need and requirement changes so that it is important that Information Technology merge with the subject in this way the subject changes as Library and Information Science. As per the demand of time it is necessary that curriculum should be change so that the students feel interest in reading. In the practical life when student enter in the competitive world they feel confident and perform well. The paper discuss about the current trends in curriculum reforms in Library and Information Science Education. The author focuses the use of social media in Libraries. Therefore it is important that the knowledge of social media is also added in the curriculum.

Keyword: LIS Education, Social Media, Library Science Curriculum

INTRODUCTION

Education is the lifelong process. Today the dimensions of the teaching are changes as from the traditional method to technical method. Information and Communication Technology (ICT) change the education pattern. In the changing scenario, the e-learning change the environment of education. The expectation of the curriculum changes as per the demand of the job market. It is the need of the environment that in curriculum designing need the attention from the higher authorities. In the previous timing, the theoretical concepts success but today the job sector force that the practical skills are important aspect and it is included in Course Curriculum of Library and Information Science in India. The practical aspects in curriculum increase the technical skills of the student. In the job market student feel confident in practical work and perform well the office environment.

LITERATURE RIVIEW

The review of related studies helps bring clarity in the subject area. The review shows that many studies were conducted to examine the curriculum in LIS Education in various universities in India.

Tripathi studied the Information Communication Technology (ICT) components in the syllabus of eight *Universities in West Bengal* which offering LIS education. The analysis concluded that IT courses introduced both in BLIS and MLIS level, the two components like computerized applications and telecommunication applications and telecommunication applications have been introduced thoroughly by all the Universities under study and balance of the both theoretical as well as practical aspects in course curricula. On the other hand Singh studied the lingering issues in LIS curriculum in

Vikram University, Ujjain. She emphasized the computer practical in BLIS and MLIS. The result is, the unawareness of students about the practical problems of the library, and after completion of the course, the students find themselves totally unfit for job market. The author also suggest that at least two hours daily should be devoted to practical work in libraries so that the students fell confident about the practical knowledge. In the same manner, Dharani Kumar, P, Biradar, B.S. and K.T. Santhose Kumar. studied the LIS curriculum and market expectation met by *DLIS, Kuvempu University.* The authors focus the LIS education just to development competent and skill human resources to meet the changing needs of this digital environment. The conclusion focuses the impact of LIS education on job market expectation by analyzing the curriculum structure of DLIS, Kuvempu University. One more study is the LIS education in *Dr. Babasaheb Ambedkar Marthwada* University is done by Sonwane and Vaishnav. The authors discussed about the BLIS four year integrated BLIS course with semester pattern for the undergraduate colleges. The introduction of this course will give the job opportunity for the candidates and if include the subject in civil services/state public services commission exams would helpful in the promotion of the subject. These promotions definitely enrich the students' participation in the LIS course.

Divatankar, Birje and Gurav studied the curriculum developments of DLIS Shivaji University at BLib&ISc and MLib&ISc Level of ICT applications and networking in libraries. The authors emphasized electronic knowledge to modernize the library services. In the ICT era, due to lack of expertise and skills, the professionals other than LIS professionals are encroaching the spheres of LIS. Therefore, it is responsibility of the LIS schools that they should generate the technically trained/ skilled LIS professionals in order to meet the present and future challenges.

The International workshops help in Tokyo as a part of the *Library and Information Professionals and Education Renewal (LIPER) Project* discusses about the major trends and issues of LIS Education in Asia Countries. The various speaker from China, Korea, Singapore, Taiwan and Thailand in order to improve understanding of recent trends in LIS Education and also emphasis for further collaboration in LIS education among Asian countries. In the workshop the common trends are identified for the LIS education in Asia like the curriculum design according to the job market, change in the core subject areas from an emphasis on manual- based collection development to ICT based information/ knowledge management and increase in the number of faculty with doctoral degrees, who prefer to teach cutting –edge courses rather than traditional library oriented courses and discussed by the author (Miwa 18).

Varalakshmi has examined the LIS education focuses on developing manpower suitable to the demands of the contemporary information environment. In the 21st century, it the need of the changing scenario of Information Technology in the LIS curriculum. The study cover the analyzing of the curriculum based on three parts to analyze study the students passed from the Department of LIS, Andhra University, Visakhapatnam from 2002-2005 and working in LICs or related field, study of LIS professionals working in higher academic institutions and special libraries seeking their opinion or various aspects of curriculum and training components and analysis of employment advertisement 2004-2005 to identify the qualifications prescribed by employers. The questionnaire methodology is used for the study. The sample size is 30 and 27 are highly encouraging respondent. The finding shows that opinion on curriculum and teaching method was that semester wise divide the IT aspect in curriculum from theoretical to practical knowledge. In the ICT skills, it is important to give the practical experience with ICTs. The experiences of the LIS professionals emphasized the study tour and projects based team works. The study marks the attention the employability demand on more IT skills, so that it is focal point in LIS curriculum (346).

Malhan and Rao views the education and training needs of Information professionals in view of the growing use of the Internet in various types of libraries and information centres. The education and training needs have resonance with the six trends reported in the Kellogg-ALISE Information Professions and Education Reform) project that are shaping LIS curriculum change according to IT environment. The present demand of LIS education and training must be planned in a way which enhances the current and further professional potential to meet varied information needs of various levels (88).

Krishan Kumar and Sharma discuss the historical perspective and growth of the subject i.e Library and Information Education in India. The author covers the Baroda School and Punjab University. In the same manner way development of LIS education by Library Association and by the Universities is also huge support for the field. The periodical growth of LIS education is also discussed here. The important aspect of Information Technology is also described as a periodical development of modernization in the subject as per the changing demand of the scenario. The author's emphasised that "Library science need to change according to the needs of the time. It is high time, librarians and teachers should come together to overcome all shortcomings and take LIS education to greater heights" (8).

On the other hand Walia consider that the historical period in LIS education, the status, the different patterns and levels of LIS education in the North India (9). Varalakshi presents an overview of LIS education in 27 LIS Departments of South India. The author analyses the course contents and suggests for innovativeness and standards to meet the present and future demands of knowledge society (19).

Gokhale in her study discusses about the changing scenario of Library and Information Science education in India is undergoing a fundamental change in its basic framework and is being re-oriented to meet the current needs of the information society. The author discusses about the programme and the different components of the LIS syllabus taught in the universities in Maharashtra. Including this also highlight towards teaching, research, and course content through regular learning. "Web-based seminars (called as Webinars) may have to be thought of as regular part of the training, as they could be cost-effective too. The Library Science schools have to take a cognisance of such emerging trends and needs of the knowledge-based society and prepare an action plan on collaborative basis" (53). The limitation of the study is will not cover the distance learning and vernacular media courses.

Panigrahi discusses about the LIS Education in east and north-eastern India covering eight states of North-eastern India like Assam, Manipur, Tripura, and soon including this Orissa and West Bengal. It is found that LIS education was started in West Bengal and spread over other states frequently. Presently, there are different levels of courses of various durations. The quality of LIS education can make library professionals fully equipped with the specialised knowledge and skills. Quality LIS education can not be operative unless proper infrastructure is developed, skilled teachers are engaged and so on. It is essential to standardisation these courses. Data related to admission requirements, course content, and course material delivery: teaching methods have been collected through questionnaire, interviews, and from respective websites. The data shows present status of today's LIS education in this region.

Education is a lifelong process. The formal education takes place in the academic institutions while informal education continues throughout the life through a wide variety of channels. Short-term courses are a necessary component in the education system because fulfills the continuing education needs of the education system. Short-term training programmer trains people to handle technology, tools, and learn routines specific to LIS profession. The history of short-term courses in LIS in India is not systematically documented. The role of national and international information systems and programmes cannot be overlooked in promoting training courses in library and information science. In the changing timing the NISCAIR, conduct a short term courses time to time for the professionals who help the professionals to cope with the recent development in LIS field (Mahesh, Narendra Kumar, and Gupta 59).

In India, library and information science education is in progress from the several years. Many government initiatives taken by different agencies have been instrumental in this development. The larger initiatives like *Radhakrishnan Commission; Kothari Commission; National Knowledge Commission* and functioning of institutions such as UGC, NAAC, DEC have influenced the entire higher education sector. The Government of India has also taken keen interest in library matters. The Advisory Committee for Libraries; Working Group of Planning Commission; National Policy on Library and Information System, etc work in the very progressive manner in subject area. UGC support the LIS education through its various committees and panels. The author discusses about the various initiatives taken by Government of India in respect of LIS education in India (Joshi 67).

Bharat Kumar studied an analysis of job advertisements during the period March-April 2010. Fifty six advertisements were collected from two national newspapers, The Times of India and The Hindustan Times, and from two job websites, Sarkari Post (http:// *www.sarkaripost.com/*) and Current Government Jobs *http://currentvacancy.blogspot.com/*). Course curriculum of four universities of North India, viz., Banaras Hindu University (BHU), Varanasi; University of Delhi (DU), Delhi; Indira Gandhi National Open University (IGNOU),Delhi; Punjab University (PU), Chandigarh was also downloaded from their respective websites to study expected competencies and the subjects taught. PU and BHU have two- years integrated MLIS course while DU and IGNOU have two separate courses (BLIS and MLIS) of one year duration. The conclusion shows that in today's competitive world, the theoretical knowledge of academic subject is not enough for LIS graduate to survive. The graduates will have to develop competencies to meet the challenging as well as changing needs of employers/users. It is important to improve their communication skills, problem solving attitude, good knowledge of IT and presentation skills. These features will enhance their employability skills.

Tripathi and Jeevan discusses the E-learning applications include web-based learning, computer-based learning, virtual classrooms, and digital collaboration. The authors highlight the various steps required to be undertaken by an institution to venture into e-learning in library and information science which has gained immense popularity in recent times. Various issues related to e-learning, which need serious attention, have been discussed here. In the same way another author Kumbhar compares the traditional education with e-learning and states that how both these methods complement each other. Asundi and Karisiddappa are suggested a new international potentiality and perspective scenario in context to developing countries like India in the field of library and information science.

Kaur and Walia in their article highlight the situation of LIS education in India with a special focus on the regions of central India. The states covered in the central India are Chhattisgarh and Madhya Pradesh. From the central region, six universities imparting LIS education were selected for their study. It was seen that these universities still have to provide an integrated two-year postgraduate course in LIS, which is being widely accepted all over the country because of its recognition by the UGC in its model curriculum. The conclusion discusses that it has become extremely vital for the universities to incorporate ICT into their curriculum both in theory as well as in practice. An internship program provides LIS students with the opportunity to gain valuable job experience during the academic year in various library operations. It helps students to acquire essential practical experience required to work in a library. The well-planned internship prepares the intern for future job responsibilities and a chance to put his knowledge to work and prepare for future job responsibilities. The growth and development of library and information professionals depends on their capacity to change traditional approach, adapt the new technology, and add new library and information services.

Varalakshmi states that library and information science education in India is nearing to celebrate centenary celebrations. However, several issues need to be resolved to meet the demands of the contemporary information society. The author discusses the growth of LIS education in India, foresees the future trends and suggest for national consensus on some of the basic issues.

In the same manner it is important that the social media related information is also added in the curriculum.

USE OF SOCIAL MEDIA IN LIBRARIES : A PRACTICAL APPROACH

The social networking sites are most popular in digital era. It become challenging in front of Library Science Professional that how to popularize the library services among users. The social media like *Face book, Twitter and Blogs* are becoming more popular among general people. Generally, the people check their Face book and Twitter account first then they check their E.mail Ids. The concept of social networking platform is the sharing of information among the clients. This is the lime light which give the new concept for Library and Information Science Professionals that how they disseminate the information, new arrival and OPAC facility at the social media site if user becomes a follower then every time he/she will be aware about the new updates of library. Even access the information at the mobile device at any time and any where.

LITERATURE REVIEW FOCUS THE IMPORTANCE OF SOCIAL MEDIA

The review of related studies helps bring clarity in the subject area. The review shows that many studies were conducted in India and abroad to examine the different aspects of use of social media or social networking sites like Face book, Twitter and Blogs etc. in libraries.

The survey was conducted in American Libraries those using Web 2.0 applications and social networking tools to promote their library programs and services. The survey cover total of 749 individuals began the survey with 548(73.2%) completing stage. Close to 62.3% of respondents represented public libraries and 23.3% represented academic libraries. The different aspects are studied during survey like purpose of using social media like marketing and promoting libraries services; use of library use Web 2.0 tools for marketing specific adult programs, quick update of user and reaching new audience of potential users etc. The funding shows that the *Face book* has had a huge impact on attractive people into our library. The users have *Face book* on their mobile devices and receive our updates on the go. The library also making the *Xtranormal* videos that talks about the library services. The *Face book* is maximum used after that *Twitter* ranked second and Blogging tools ranked third (Rogers). Another survey conducted with the focus point to determine the awareness and use of web 2.0 tools by librarians in *Anambra State in Nigeria.* The questionnaire was designed and distributed to all professional librarians in the state who are member of the *Nigerian Library Association.* The result shows a low awareness and use of web 2.0 tools by the librarians. The computer expertise, motivation, lack of facilities and access restriction are among the impediments to the librarians' use of web 2.0 tools (Anunobi and Ogbonna).

The use of *Twitter* by the modern libraries to disseminate informative/knowledge to their users was studied by the authors. The objective of the study is to find out whether *Twitter* is used for social networking in the libraries of the United States of America (U.S.)? Which way libraries in U.S. are using *Twitter*? What important is communicated through Twitter? Whether U.S Library *Twitter* accounts have any followers? The methodology applied for the study is a survey of the entire universe of *Twitter* accounts of U.S. Libraries that are found in websites like *Lindy Brown's Blog.* The findings shows that U.S. Libraries use Twitter to provide alerts and current awareness services to their users Library Twitter accounts are not followed by encouraging number of followers. It is the community building technologies of the Web 2.0 that need to be utilized to the optimum extent by the libraries to develop scholarly communities (Vishwa Mohan and Munigal). On the other hand the developing technology skills for *Academic Librarians in University in*

Kerala were studied in deep manner. The objective of the study is to analyses the skills and awareness of library professionals in an electronic environment. The study is based on a questionnaire survey of library professionals employed in the central and department libraries of the seven major *Universities of Kerala.* Use of Web Tools and services is also considered as one of the objective in the study. Regarding this aspect the result shows that E. mail, instant messaging or chat are frequently used by 85.9% of professionals. *Wiki* used by 69.1% and after that *Discussion groups* known by 42.8% of professionals. In addition, a social network site was used daily by 41.6% professionals. *You Tube, Flickr and Web logs* are used by the professionals. The *RSS feeds* and content management systems used by very few professionals. The application of the Web Tools is yet to be popular in University Libraries (Susan and Baby).

Social networking sites are most popular among young generation. Smith-Yoshimuru and Shein discusses about The *Library Thing,* which is a social media site that enables users to create online collections of books; rate, tag and review books; add biographical information about authors and add image of authors and book covers. The *Library Thing* is used by bibliophiles worldwide to manage their personal libraries and track their own reading activities, but is also used by a number of small libraries and museums as a cost- effective way to catalog their holding and enable their staff and user to tag and review their holdings. *Library Thing for Libraries (LTFL)* is a related, but separate service that adds Web 2.0 features to an institution existing Online Public Access Catalogue (OPAC) and repurposes user- contributed images and other materials from the Library Thing to enrich the OPAC. The LTFL services are used by more than 1,600 public and academic libraries throughout the world. The LTFL services to enhance their OPACs and enables users to interact with their collections (1-3, 174).

The value of social network and to appreciate the initiative taken by *IFLA Action for Development through Libraries Program (ALP)* is providing a platform for this joint effort. The Web 2.0 environment including weblogs, wikis and syndications provide the more interactive user centered library and information services. The weblogs is a tool that libraries can use to promote their services or to provide a means of communication with their users (Namila Suraweera et al.).

Social media is about sharing, learning, conversations and giving information. *Vikram Sarabhai Library* on *Facebook, Twitter* and *Wikipedia.* The social media sites are free of cost, easy to use, reach to large audience, real time information sharing network, easy to get feedback of users, library can use for promotional activities and more informal source friendly for communicating with user better than going traditional way. It is important that the setting up library social media account, link to the library website, create a welcoming and informal description of the library and including always options for customization. The upload aspect on social media covers library news and events; new additions to your collection links to articles, videos etc. Community information; solicit feedback means why do user use the library; respond to people; pictures like events, library photos and anything else that know your community (Navik and Amin).

Noushia Praveen studied the use of social networking site *(Face book)* in making awareness among the library and information science professionals of University libraries of Uttar Pradesh. The author collected data from questionnaire that was circulated among the LIS professionals randomly. The survey of social networking site i.e. *Face book* in making awareness among LIS professionals. The analysis will help the professionals in deriving the benefits of social networking site, face book proves helpful in generating awareness about current happenings, professional information, job opportunities and educational development. The analysis result shows the 60% respondent opinion is that *Face book* proves helpful in making awareness and 55% LIS professional were use *Face book* everyday and 52% respondent were agreeing that *Face book* works as platform to avoid barriers of location and nationality (9-17).

In the same manner new focus point in digital environment is the digital collection marketing in the social media. The digital librarians can cultivate a broader awareness of their collections is through social networking. The social networking site provides a way for digital librarian to develop conversation with users, extent general awareness of the digital collection, and establish the librarian as a knowledgeable, helpful and easy accessible source of authoritative information regarding a given subject area. The important aspect to prove the value of their collection by establishing themselves as essential participant in relevant knowledge-creating conversation (Schrier).

A user survey was conducted with basic web 2.0 related questions. The survey conducted on the usage of web 2.0 services especially for libraries. The objectives of the study are the level of various web 2.0 services used by the library practitioners, the understanding of various web 2.0 services pertaining to libraries, what makes the library professionals to use the web 2.0 services, the specific library applications pertaining to web 2.0 used and the challenges that face in using web 2.0 services. The survey was conducted through the web based questionnaire posted at *ETTLIS@Ning Social networking site*. A total number of 452 responses were collected through this survey. 67.6%of respondents were from *India, followed by USA, Paskistan, Malaysia and Srilanka*. The finding shows that 83% of the respondents are well aware of the web 2.0. The most popular are *Blogs* among 59% of the respondents have either used or they are aware of followed by social networking such as *news feeds, instant messaging, streaming media and tagging.* Close to 35% of the respondents believe that due to the change in information seeking behavior of the users and close to 25% of the users felt that current trends in information processing, retrieval and dissemination guides towards the usage of web 2.0 tools and technologies. The *Face book* and *Orkut* remains the favorite's social networking sites among 50% of the library professionals. Close to 69% of the respondents clearly shows how social networking sites are becoming marketing and awareness creating tools for libraries. The survey concluded that this kind of survey is helpful for the Library and Information Science Professionals in providing guidance and assistance to better the services (Shri Ram et. al).

McGrath, Rogers and Gilligan have studied the level of provision of young people in Irish public library services and to ascertain the views of young people on issues and opportunities affecting them. The questionnaire meeting with library professionals and focus group discussion method is used for collecting the views of the users. In all 32 cities and country library authorities were surveyed and 91% responded. In additional 154 young people participated in *focus group discussions.* In the public library there are several factors that encourage the library use. The promotion of library services is difficult task for the LIS professionals. But many libraries have now embraced the Internet and social networking sites in order to promote their services and link or connect with younger users. The best example of good practice is found in the *USA Internet access* is widely available throughout the *King County Library system.* Access to social networking sites, such as *MySpace or Face book,* is freely available. In fact, the library itself has a page on *My Space,* linked to the library websites (*www.kcls.org*). The teen page on the library website promotes events for young people and provides an online *'Ask a Librarian' resources* '(1-39).

Krishnamurthy and Lalitha in their article explore the Library 2.0 a term that provides focus to a number of ongoing discussions centered on how libraries should make themselves and their services visible to end users and to one another. The social networking sites provide a platform free of charge for users to share exciting contents. The sites evolved from the concept of sharing information. Libraries and Librarians have increasing been exploring social networking sites for both personal and professional resources (238-88).

Starr highlights the *California Digital Library* (CDL) established a *Twitter* account in 2009. The author focus a key feature of the approach has been to reuse content from the CDL Newsletter and to automate most of the administration, making it nearly maintenance free (23-8).

The author conducted a survey in the member libraries of *Business Librarians Association.* The survey fit into four groups: about you, use of general Web 2.0 tools, use of specific web 2.0 tool and final comments. The survey conducted online using the forms features of *Google Docs.* The finding shows that the majority of respondent involve in the use of Web 2.0. The results have been used by the *BLA Committee* to guide the development of a social media workshop for BLA members. It is hoped that BLA members will be able to use this survey and the materials from the workshops, when developing a strategy for the introduction of new Web 2.0 services (Cragg).

The modern academic libraries which fulfill the advance demand of the users in the online environment largely supported by web 2.0 technologies. Blogs can be used as library information and publicity tool, feedback instrument, interactive and collaborative learning medium and as a facility for library promotion. The author focus that the reaching the user at their own time and space is more easy and productive when we adapt new web technologies. The *Library Kendriya Vidiyalaya Pattom* available at *Blog* and *Face book.* The home works and assignments online available on *Kendriya Vidiyalaya Pattom*(Shift 1) Thiruvananthapuram, Kerala. *My Dear Book Blog* and *Library kv Pattom Tvm* is also popular among users. The library uses *Twitter* to convey short messages regarding its resources (*New Book Alters,* etc.) and services. Web 2.0 is an opportunity that should and can be harnessed for the academic achievement of the students and make the library an entity that matters (Faisal).

Naslund and Giustini have studied *California School Library Association* (CSLA) is learning 2.0 which includes 23 activities and was built using *Blogger, Flickr* (photo-sharing), *Odeo* (podcasting), *You Tube Videos, PB wiki* (hosted wikisite) and *Bloglines* (an *RSS reader).* Each tutorial begins with exercise that exposes participants to a variety of tools and sites. The *Blogs, Library Thing* (social cataloguing), *Wikis, Google Docs, Zoho Writer, and Delicious* using their own Blogs, participants and post comments about what they are learning. The opportunity to experiment with social software, and engage in exploration, gives the high priority for teacher librarians interested in school library 2.0 (55-67).

CONCLUSION

The current trends in Library and Information Science force the higher authorities that they pay their attention in designing the LIS curriculum as per the demand of job sector. It is also important that the Universities follow the uniformity in curriculum. The theoretic parts are important but not neglect the practical part of the subject.. The knowledge of social networking site is important in the LIS education curriculum. In this manner in the future students use social networking sites as a most alternative tool for marketing the library collection in digital platform. The Face book, Twitter and

Blogs make the path easy for the library professionals but sad to say that most of the professionals don't know about the Web 2.0 environment. In the developing network era they don't want to adopt a new technology. It is important that the changing demand of the users' is fulfill only when we give the services in which they feel comfortable. The *FOURTH LAW* Library Science "*SAVE THE TIME OF THE USER*" fulfill means they access the social media site, meet their friends, access the library, ask a query and post a comment at one place. In other words we can say that multipurpose solve at one platform means *SAVE THE TIME OF THE USER.*

REFERENCE

- **Asundi, A.Y. and Karisiddappa, C.R.** "Library and Information Science Education in India: International Perspectives with Special Reference to Developing Countries." *DESIDOC Journal of Library & Information Technology* 27, 2 (2007): 5-11 Print.
- **Bharat Kumar.** "Employability of Library and Information Science Graduates: Competencies Expected versus Taught—a Case Study." *DESIDOC Journal of Library & Information Technology* 30, 5 (2010): 74-82. Print.
- **Dharani Kumar, P, Biradar, B.S. and K.T. Santhose Kumar.** " LIS Curriculum and Market Expectation: a study with special reference to LIS Curriculum, Kuvempu University." *Emerging Challenges and Lingering Issues in LIS Education, Research and Training. Proceedings of the 27th IATLIS 2010, Patiala. Nov 17-19, 2010.* Eds. Jagtar Singh and Trishanjit Kaur. Patiala: Dept. of Library and Information Science, Punjabi University, 2010. 72-81. Print.
- **Divtankar, N.I., Birje, S.R. and Gurav, D.S**. " Curriculum development in the light of ICT applications and networking in libraries: a Case Study of DLIS, Shivaji University, Kolhapur." *Emerging Challenges and Lingering Issues in LIS Education, Research and Training. Proceedings of the 27th IATLIS 2010, Patiala. Nov 17-19, 2010.* Eds. Jagtar Singh and Trishanjit Kaur. Patiala: Dept. of Library and Information Science, Punjabi University, 2010.89-100. Print.

- **Gokhale, P.** "Library and Information Science Education in Maharashtra: A Perspective." *DESIDOC Journal of Library & Information Technology* 30, 5 (2010): 48-55.Print.
- **Joshi, M. K.** "Library and Information Science Education in India: Some Government Initiatives." *DESIDOC Journal of Library & Information Technology* 30, 5 (2010):67-73.Print.
- **Krishan Kumar and Sharma, J.** "Library and Information Science Education in India: A Historical Perspective." *DESIDOC Journal of Library & Information Technology* 30, 5 (2010): 3-8. Print.
- **Kumbhar, R**. "Use of E-learning in Library and Information Science Education." *DESIDOC Journal of Library & Information Technology* 29, 1 (2009): 37-41 Print.
- **Mahesh, G, Narendra Kumar, Gupta, D. K.** "Short-term Library and Information Science Training Courses in India." *DESIDOC Journal of Library & Information Technology* 30, 5 (2010): 56-60.Print.
- **Malhan, I.V and Rao, Shivarama.** "The Networking Information Environment: implications for education of library and information professionals." *Malaysian Journal of Library and Information Science* 11, 1 (2006): 75-88.
- **Miwa, M**. "Trends and issues of LIS education in Asia." *Library and Information Education and Practice 2006. Proceedings of the Asia-Pacific Conference (A-LIEP 2006), Singapore. April 3-6, 2006.* Ed. C. Khoo, D. Singh and A.S. Chaudhry. Singapore: School of Communication and Information, Nanyang Technological University, 2006. 18-26. Print.
- **Panigrahi, P.** "Library and Information Science Education in East and North-East India: Retrospect and Prospects." *DESIDOC Journal of Library & Information Technology* 30, 5 (2010): 32-47.Print.
- **Singh, S.** "Lingering issues in LIS Curriculum: A Case Study of Vikram University, Ujjain." *Emerging Challenges and Lingering Issues in LIS Education, Research and Training. Proceedings of the 27th IATLIS 2010, Patiala. Nov 17-19, 2010.* Eds. Jagtar Singh and Trishanjit Kaur. Patiala: Dept. of Library and Information Science, Punjabi University, 2010. 66-71. Print.
- **Sonwane, S.S, Vaishnav, A.V.** " LIS Curriculum Development for Undergraduate Level: A Case Study." *Emerging Challenges and Lingering Issues in LIS Education, Research and Training.*

Proceedings of the 27th IATLIS 2010, Patiala. Nov 17-19, 2010. Eds. Jagtar Singh and Trishanjit Kaur. Patiala: Dept. of Library and Information Science, Punjabi University, 2010. 82-88. Print.

- **Tripathi, Manorama and Jeevan, V.K.J.** "e-Learning Library and Information Science: A Pragmatic View for India." *DESIDOC Journal of Library & Information Technology* 30, 5 (2010):83-90. Print.
- **Tripathi, T.** "Recent Trends of LIS Education in the Universities in West Bengal: Analysis on ICT in Curricula and Associated Facilities." *Emerging Challenges and Lingering Issues in LIS Education, Research and Training. Proceedings of the 27th IATLIS 2010, Patiala. Nov 17-19, 2010.* Eds. Jagtar Singh and Trishanjit Kaur. Patiala: Dept. of Library and Information Science, Punjabi University, 2010. 60-65. Print.
- **Varalakshmi, R.S.R.** "Educating 21st century LIS professionals- The needs and expectations: A survey of Indian LIS professionals and alumni." *Library and Information Education and Practice 2006Proceedings of the Asia-Pacific Conference (A-LIEP 2006), Singapore. April 3-6, 2006.* Ed. C. Khoo, D. Singh and A.S. Chaudhry. Singapore: School of Communication and Information, Nanyang Teachological University, 2006. 338-46. Print.
- "Library and Information Science Education in South India: Perspective and Challenges." *DESIDOC Journal of Library & Information Technology* 30, 5 (2010): 19-31Print.
- "Need for National Consensus on Library and Information Science Education in India." *DESIDOC Journal of Library & Information Technology* 27, 2 (2007): 13-20 Print.
- **Walia, P.K.** "Library and Information Science Education in North India." *DESIDOC Journal of Library & Information Technology* 30, 5 (2010): 9-18.Print.
- **Kaur, P.** "Library and Information Science Education in Chhattisgarh and Madhya Pradesh." *DESIDOC Journal of Library & Information Technology* 30, 5 (2010): 91-96 Print.
- **Anunobi, C.V. and Ogbonna, A.U.** "Web 2.0 Use by Librarians in a State in Nigeria" *Developing Country Studies* 2.5(2012) Print.
- **Cragg, Emma**. "Use of Social Media in the Member Libraries of the Business Librarian Association." 2010. Web. 6 June. 2012.

- **Faisal, S.L.** "Blogs and Online Social Networks as User Centric Services Tools in Academic Libraries: An Indian Library Experience. ICAL 2009." Web. 10 June. 2012.
- **Krishnamurthy M and Lalitha, Ashwath.** "Social Network Technology and Its implications for Libraries: Transforming the Library Services through the Web." *SRELS Journal of Information Management* 47.3(2010):238-88. Print.
- **Naslund, Jo- Anne and Giustini, Dean.** "Towards School Library 2.0: An introduction to Social Software tools for Teacher Librarians". *School Libraries Worldwide.* 14.2 (2008): 55-67. Print.
- **Navik, Viral and Amin, Jignesh.** "Effective use of Social Media / Networks Tools for Marketing of Library and Information Products and Services: Face book, Twitter and Wikipedia". Web. 12 June. 2012.
- **Noushia Praveen.** "Use of Social Networking Site (Facebook) in making awareness among the Library and Information Science Professionals of University Libraries of U.P: A Case Study". *International Journal of Digital Library Services* 1.1(2011): 9-17. Print.
- **Rogers, C.R.** *American Libraries are using New Tools for Public Relations and to Attract New Users –Fourth Annual Survey November 2011.* Columbia: South Carolina, 2012. Print.
- **Starr, John.** "California Digital Library in Twitter- Land." *Computers in Libraries –West port* Sept (2010): 23-8. Print.
- **Smith- Yoshimuru, Karen and Shein, Cyndi.** *Social Meta data for Libraries, Archives and Museums Part 1: Site Reviews.* USA: OCLC Research, 2011. 1-174. Print.
- **Shri Ram, Kataria, Sanjay, Paliwal, Nitin and Hopkinson, Alan.** "Acceptance and Usage of Web 2.0 services in libraries: A Survey." Emerging Technologies and Changing Dimensions of Libraries and Information Services. 3-5 June. 2010, Wakhnaghat. Eds. Sanjay Kataria, John Paul Anbu K and Shri Ram. New Delhi: KBD, 2010. Web. 5 July. 2012.
- **Mc Grath, Brid, Rogers, Margaret and Gilligan, Robbie.** *Young People and Public Libraries in Ireland: Issues and Opportunities.* Dublin: Children and Youth Affairs, 2012. 1-39. Print.
- **Schrier, R.A.** "Digital Librarianship & Social Media: The Digital Library as Conversation Facilitator." *D-Lib Magazine* 17.7-8 (2011). Web. 10 June. 2012.

- **Susan, M.K. and Baby, M.D.** "Developing Technology skills for Academic Librarians: A Study Based on the Universities in Kerala, India." *Library Philosophy and Practice* (2012). Web 10 July 2012
- **Namila Suraweera, S.A.D.H, Razali, Norhayati, Chouhan, Lal Bahadur, Tamang, Neela, Hubilla, A.M.K.U, Ratnayake, A.R.M.M, Rubosa, N.C, Malik, F.A and Mahesar, S.N.** "Value of Social Networking in Libraries and Information organizations in Asia and Oceania". Open access to knowledge - promoting sustainable progress. 10-15 August 2010, Gothenburg. Web. 8 July 2010.
- **Vishwa Mohan, V and Munigal, Achala.** "Use of community Building Web Technologies in Libraries: A study of Twitter in American Libraries." *Informing Science and Information T echnology Education Conference (InSITE). 22-27June. 2012, Canada.* Eds. Eli Cohen and Elizabeth Boyd. USA: Informing Science Institute, 2012. 205-21. Print.

14

Digitisation Issues in NIFT: Prospects and Problems

Rajnish Tamrakar
National Instituteof Fashion Technology, NIFT Block, M.P. Bhoj Open University Campus, Kolar Road, Bhopal- 462 016 (M.P.)

Neerja Verma
Professor & Head, DLIS, M.L.B. Govt. College of Excellence, Gwalior-474 009 (M.P.)

ABSTRACT

Due to technological invasion, majority of libraries are getting converted themselves into digital libraries which are more suitable to fulfil their basic objectives of preserving the scientific, National heritage and culture and making it globally accessible by passing all constraints of time and space. Digitisation has changed the entire concept of R & D activities and the ways scholars, students and a common user access and use scholarly information. This paper broadly covers digitisation issues in National Institute of Fashion Technology (NIFT), its need for library to meet users' needs, problem areas of IPRs and copyright, preservation etc. It also covers advantages, problems in digitisation at NIFT level.

Keywords : Digitisation, digital library, copyright, IPR, NIFT, fashion technology.

INTRODUCTION

It is an easy task for an individual to store and recover a particular document when the collection of documents is small but when the collection rises, the archival and retrieval process becomes tedious and time consuming. Due to the changing technologies innovations, the paper media is becoming outdated and not able to support the formats that computer technology is supporting i.e. audio, visual etc. In present scenario, libraries are providing access to information by using digital libraries in their day-to-day activities. The recent developments in the area of computers and networks namely internet, intranet and DVDs have brought radical changes in the process of generating, storage, retrieval and dissemination of information. The digital library has been one of the important outputs of rapid changes in web technology allowing user to access information from any where in the world.

Today, all libraries of NIFT situated in different parts of country are providing digital library services to their users as well as outsiders. In-spite of large number of developments in the area of digitisation, it is observed that the fashion/ textile professionals, designers are not satisfied with the digital library services. The professionals feel urgent need for development of fashion library covering core area of textile/ fashion technology. This is needed to provide relevant information in multi-disciplinary subjects and to bring web services of all library of NIFT on a single platform.

RATIONALE BEHIND DIGITISATION

The objective of library digitisation is to develop information system providing access to a coherent collection of material, which will be in digital format, and to fully exploit the opportunities that are offered by the materials that are in digital formats. There is, in reality, a continuity between traditional library roles and missions and the objectives of digital library systems. The main reasons behind digitisation of libraries can be summarised as:

- To provide efficiently both personalised and retrospective services in efficient manner.
- To collect, manipulate and disseminate information.
- To make timely and easily availability of all publications.
- To have large number of databases in CDs.
- To serve widely dispersed communities throughout the network.
- To avoid routine jobs and save the time of library professionals.

WHAT IS DIGITISATION?

The digitisation is the process of translating a piece of information such as books, journal article, sound recording, pictures, audio tapes or video recordings etc, into bits. Turning information into these binary digits (bits) is called digitisation, which can be accomplished through a variety of technologies. According to "Witten and Bridge" 2003, digitisation is the process of taking traditional library materials that are in form of books and papers, and converting them to the electronic form where they can be stored and manipulated by a computer.

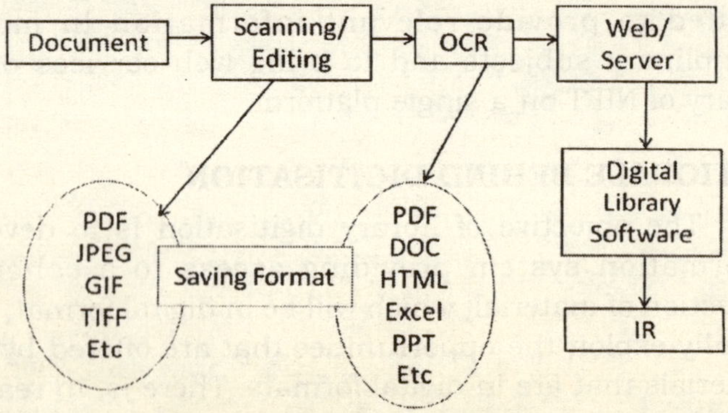

Fig. 1. Digitisation Process

PROFILE OF NATIONAL INSTITUTE OF FASHION TECHNOLOGY

National Institute of Fashion Technology was set up in 1986 under the aegis of the Ministry of Textiles, Government of India to emerge as a centre of excellence and innovation, proactively catalysing growth of fashion business through leadership in professional education with concern for social and human values. It has emerged as the premier Institute of design, management and technology, developing professionals for taking up leadership positions in fashion business in the emerging global scenario. The Institute is a pioneer in envisioning and evolving fashion business education in the country through a network of fifteen professionally managed centres viz. Bangalore, Bhopal, Bhubaneswar, Chennai, Gandhinagar, Hyderabad, Jodhpur, Kangra, Kannur, Kolkatta, Mumbai, New Delhi, Patna, Raibareli, Shillong. NIFT is the first premier Institute in the world to award its own degrees in the field of education of fashion technology.

The libraries of NIFT are known as Resource Centre. The Resource Centre in each NIFT centre provides the necessary infrastructure to collate and disseminate this critical input. The network of NIFT Resource Centres is the only fashion information system in India serving the fashion professionals, would-be professionals and fashion educators. Its integrated collection of print, visual and creative material resources is the only systematically documented source of information available in India for study of International and contemporary Indian fashion. The system is a decentralized network, partially automated and is coordinated by the National Resource Centre (NRC) at NIFT, New Delhi. There are two wings in Resource Centre, library wing and the material wing. The Library wing of the Resource Centre comprises the print and non-print information sources. The library wing of Resource Centre have a rich collection of books and non-book materials covering the core areas of study such as textiles, fashion design, history of costumes and fashion, accessories, apparel construction, International trade, marketing and management. Besides, the material wing of the Resource Centre contains of textiles, costumes, accessories, swatches, fabrics etc.

COLLECTION OF NIFT LIBRARIES:

Most of the libraries are having some unique materials, manuscripts, historic documents, personal documents in addition to these NIFTs libraries having costumes, textile and accessories of Indian as well as foreign origin, slides and other rare materials. Such materials need due attention for their preservation and making them serviceable. All these materials are most valuable source of information for fashion industry, it reveals the past events and trends to students to understand the concepts of old fashion, costumes, culture, style of living etc. Slides depicting artwork, architecture and cultural objects are typically used for the study, teaching and documentation of art history, architectural history and visual culture. Digitisation is an answer to such type of materials and problems. However, it is easy to digitise white, clean opaque paper whereas costumes, fabrics, accessories, craft documentation, slides and other rare non print materials are really difficult to digitise.

DIGITISATION ISSUES AT NIFT

All the libraries of NIFT are providing digital library services to their students, faculty members, outsiders etc over last few years. But the library users feel that digital library services are not able to fully meet the requirements of the students, industry members. This is true that NIFT is yet to establish digitisation on sound grounds. Some of the problems faced by the NIFT libraries are as under:

- Lack of adequate infrastructure, the libraries do not have adequate infrastructure like physical computing facilities, hardware, software, scanning equipment or trained, skilful manpower to initiate and execute digitisation projects. It is widely accepted that a great deal of time, money and staff commitment is required for starting and implementing digitisation projects.
- The digitisation policies of the libraries accord low priority to the NPM like costumes, garments, fabrics, swatches etc as compared to the books and other reading materials.
- NIFT web OPAC does not provide the information about the e-resources procured/ developed in various libraries of NIFT, and
- Present availability of e-documents does not support R & D in multidisciplinary area of work.
- Number of coverage of e-journals procured by individually library is rather low.
- Competent authority does not accept procurement of journals in e-version alone.
- Diversity of materials like costumes, garments, fabrics, yarns etc.

INITIATIVES TAKEN BY NIFT

Libraries of NIFT are providing access to digital information adopting following methods:

- By subscribing to various online databases (e-journals, online indexing and abstracting services etc).
- Downloading key information from internet (e-books, forecasts, technical reports, newspaper clippings etc).
- Scan and digitisation of documents in key areas of work, rare books etc by using suitable retrieval software.

- NIFT libraries are having good collection of materials like costumes, textile, accessories, fabrics, designers' garments which are widely used by the faculty for teaching and for reference by students and industry. Keeping in view users' requirements, projects in progress and future areas of work, National Resource Centre (NRC), NIFT HO has initiated creation and development of fashion information system.

INTELLECTUAL PROPERTY RIGHTS AND COPYRIGHT ISSUES

Intellectual Property (IP) pertains to any original creation of the human intellect such as artistic, literary, technical or scientific creation. Intellectual Property Rights (IPR) refers to the legal rights given by the state to the inventor/creator to protect his invention/creation for a certain period of time. These legal rights confer an exclusive right to the inventor/creator or his/her assignee to fully utilize his/her invention/creation for a given period of time.

IMPORTANCE OF IP IN THE FIELD OF INNOVATION AND FASHION

The world has always accepted and continues to acknowledge, the role 'knowledge' plays as one of the major evolving factors of the human life and society. One way of securing and trading knowledge is through Intellectual Property Rights System. This is because new and original ideas find creative expressions by the innovative and intelligent use of an inherent knowledge base. It is easy, then, to see how and why 'knowledge' has become the focal point of property rights.

The current importance of IPRs is dictated by the following reasons:

- Technologies are changing rapidly.

- Product life cycle is becoming shorter.
- Investments on R&D, production, marketing have become very high.
- Human resources should possess high level of skills and
- The industry is becoming very competitive.

Copyright-apart from the copyrightable material of students' works, NIFT as an organisation needs to safeguard documents which are intrinsic to its working. Examples can be:

- Projects undertaken by students as part of their graduation/ post graduation.
- Projects undertaken by the faculty as part of their academic structure.
- Administrative documents like the student manual, the academic manual etc.
- A promotional material including contents on its websites.
- Information materials for NIFT- brochures, leaflets etc.
- Study materials developed by faculty as part of their work profile.

CONCLUSION

Today a large number of libraries are undertaking digitisation projects to provide global access to materials in their collections and long term preservation of these materials. Digitisation involves the process of converting print and other materials into digital form. Digital form of documents is created through a variety of technologies. NIFT is committed to provide information services to its users using latest ICT. Fashion technology has better utility of ICT in terms of creation, storage and dissemination of information. NIFT also has undertaken a project to digitise the costumes, textiles and accessories of Indian as well as foreign origin in the collection of its libraries.

REFERENCES

- Venkatesh, N, Rao GV Ramana and Kalpavalli, S. (2008). Digitisation issues in DRDO- prospects and problems, Proceedings of National conference on digitisation and digital preservation held at DESIDOC, New Delhi, December, 2008, pp. 3-7.
- Arora, Jagdish (2009), Digitisation anu digital preservation. DESIDOC journal of library and information technology. Vol. 29, No. 2, pp. 82.84.
- Mani, NS (2009), Digitisation: preservation and challenges. DESIDOC journal of library and information technology. Vol. 29, No. 1, pp. 69-71.
- Ravi, B. (2008). University of Hyderabad library-digitisation project. Proceedings of National conference on digitisation and digital preservation held at DESIDOC, New Delhi, December, 2008, pp. 8-13.
- IPR manual (2011). National Institute of Fashion Technology. New Delhi.
- Witten Ian, H. and Bridge David, Brain. *How to build a digital library*. London, Morgan Publication.

15

Emerging Trends of Library and Information Science Education in India

Neeraj Kumar
Assistant Professor, D.S.College, Gangtok (Sikkim)
Ajay Pandey
Research Scholar, APS University, Rewa

INTRODUCTION

In a common parlance Library and Information Science Education is understood to be an organic entity, which changes and grow with time, responding to variety of needs and requirements of society. It has been the tool of operation for a doctor, a measuring instrument for an engineer, an ornament in the agriculture field and a factor of economic development. The 20th century had been revolutionary in the educational field and the 21st century has promised for more sophisticated and effective educational system through the use of educational technology. But alongside the pace of change in educational scenario a contrary development is also taking place mostly in terms of erosion of educational values.

LIS Education in India has been playing a very

important role in shaping the youths of the nation in the field of information dissemination, and storing the knowledge services. LIS education is under the higher education system and Indian higher education system is one of the largest education systems in world with over 15 million students and half a million of teachers. LIS educational institutions provide the necessary trained and educated manpower required for the development of library and information center needed for the growth and development of a nation. LIS education is a powerful tool to create and disseminate the knowledge for an information based society.

After the 100 years journey of LIS education in India has progressed well in terms of institutions, teachers and enrolment of students. In higher education, presently more than 500 universities and 27000 colleges, this is an increase of 24 times in case of universities and 52 times in case of colleges since independence. There has been a considerable improvement in terms of gross enrolment ration from less than 1 year in early 1950s to over 15 years now. But it is still very low compared to 24.2% of the world average. There is a far difference between India and individual countries. For the enrolment example ratio of the students of higher education in Canada is 89%, USA 82.9%, Australia 80.8%, UK 54% and France 52%. Even a developing country like Thailand is in a better position than India where GER in higher education is about 21%. Therefore, there is a need to expand the intake capacity if the country is to achieve a target of 25.2% GER in higher education. Now, one of the most important issues before the higher education system in our country is enhancing access to higher education so that a knowledge based society can be built. Therefore after independence the expansion of higher education was the top priority of India. At present (as of March 2013) India has 40 central universities, 234 state universities 21 state private universities but appropriately 70%

institutions are providing LIS education.

There are various kinds of emerging trends in LIS education, which are bringing about technological advancements responsible for rapid growth and development of our country.

GLOBALIZATION

Globalization refers to the rapid development of technology finance, trade, knowledge, values and ideas the borders. It also refers to global competition and changes occurring in a competitive world of late remarkable changes are occurring all over the world which shows that no ration can remain in isolation. Globalization and socio-economic integration are perceived in terms of opening up of liberal movement of society of goods, services and factors of production. LIS education systems, policies and institutions are being transformed by globalization which is widening; deepening and speeding up of worldwide inter connecters. The changing nature of LIS education is increasingly dependent upon knowledge disseminate base society moving towards advance technology system.

Globalization is a newly emerging phenomenon. It has been defined as a set of process by which the world is rapidly being integrated into one economic space via increased international trade, which is further internationalized by production and financial market. Globalization is also referred to as one-world or open world. It makes communication easier, bring people together.

LIS education as a service oriented sector is a part of globalization process under the general agreement of trade and tariff (GATT).

Under GATT, globalization is defined as:

a. Cross border delivery

b. Consumption abroad

c. Commercial presence

d. Movement of natural persons.

This relates to technical, professional and other type of education services.

The basic objective of globalization is to enhance productivity and to make the educational system an instrument for preparing students, who can complete in the world markets as productive members of the society. It also refers to integrating teaching, learning and service functions of institutions in an international dimension.

Now, with new technology, knowledge is easily portable and lends itself to globalization. It leads to the creation and application of new knowledge to a wide range of human activities through the use of ICT. In other words, the world as a whole is passing through a knowledge revolution therefore a country without good quality education may become isolated in the global knowledge based economy. Knigh and Ede-wit defines globalization as "the flow of technology, economy, knowledge, people, values and ideas across brooders. Globalization affects each country in a different way due to nation's individual's history, traditions, culture and priorities".

The process of Globalization had a great impact on education :

- With the unification of LIS education better global expansion is possible.
- Quality has substantially improved.
- Students from all round the world have easy access to LIS education.
- Diversified courses are available now.
- Developing countries are benefitting.
- International standards are maintained.
- ICT has further enhanced globalization.
- Mobility of teachers from reputed universities

thereby bringing more information and quality in teaching.

Therefore, Globalization should be viewed as the deepening relationships and broadening interdependence among people from different countries, an opportunity and challenge. In globalization LIS education should have quality, standards in terms of knowledge, skills and competences in different fields which can directly create national wealth. LIS education system in India should be able to create commercialization, in the sense that it can sell and purchase in the market. It should have market values. Educational product should be saleable in global market. This a new trend which can create a global economy

DISTANCE EDUCATION

Distance education or distance learning is a field of education that focuses on teaching methods and technology with the aim of delivering teaching, after on an individual basis, to students who are not physically present in a traditional educational setting such as a classroom. It has been described as "a process to create and provide access to learning when the source of information and the learners are separated by time and distance or both". This is a dominant mode of education now a day it was first taken by CABE in 1961 by appointing a committee under the chairmanship of Professor D.S. Kothari. In India it is offered by:-

i. Formal Universities

ii. State Open Universities

iii. IGNOU – Apex body for distance and open education.

The following some reasons for embrace of distance learning:-

Expanding access : Distance education can assist in meeting the demand for education and training demand from the general populace and businesses, especially because it offers the possibility of a flexibility to accommodate the many time constraints imposed by personal responsibilities and commitments.

Alleviate Capacity Constraints : Mostly or entirely conducted off-site, the system reduces the demand on institutional infrastructure such as buildings.

Making Money from Emerging Markets : Globally acceptance of the value of lifelong learning, beyond the normal period and institutions can benefit financially from this by adopting distance education sectors of education such as courses for business executives as being "more lucrative than traditional markets".

Therefore, it is noticed that today, distance education is emerging as a necessary alternative to formal education system throughout the globe. It can satisfy learners who want to climb up the ladder of education even while they are working.

QUALITY ASSURANCE

India is a developing country in the world, with an annual growth rate more than 9%. In order to sustain the growth rate, there is need to increase the number of institutions and also the quality of higher education in India. The quality for education during the 12th 5 year plan represents a fourfold increase over the previous plan and stands more than 2500 billion. Therefore, in order to ensure satisfactory level of quality in the functioning of the large number of diverse higher educational institutions. The quality of education imparted by them has to be assured.

The higher education sector ensures quality of the educational process with the help of accreditation agencies established for the purpose. The various accreditation agencies are as follows:

INFORMATION AND COMMUNICATION TECHNOLOGY (ICT)

The information and communication technology (ICT) is a diverse set of technological tools and resources used to accommodate and to create, disseminate, store and manage information. It accommodates any communication device or application for example radio, television, computer, hard ware and soft ware, satellite systems etc.

Basically ICT can be categorized into five main types:

- e-Learning
- u-Learning
- Blended learning
- Digital learning
- Personalized learning

E-learning

E-learning or electronic learning is associated with the field of advanced learning technology (ADL). It is basically linked to technologies and associated methodologies in learning using multi-media technology. This covers a wide set of applications right from web-paging to virtual classroom to digital collaboration. E-learning can be used widely in open and formal education. It is very much in demand in distance education as it overcomes timing, attendance and travel difficulties. Videoed lectures are much talked about in e-learning.

U-learning

Ubiquitous learning or u-learning more commonly known as "every where learning" i.e. learning follows people e.g. – internet learning. Which work related or personal learning is required. Various devices can be used to retreat the information in an appropriate format e.g. – cell phones, Ipads, Ipods, Academia MP3, Digital books, Pen drives, Teleconferencing i.e. Audio, Audio-Video,

Video, Computers, e-mail, etc. Ubiquitous learning is an adaptation of e-learning. Therefore, it is very flexible i.e. learning takes place anywhere, anytime and context. Mobile learning in e-learning has brought in a major transformation in education.

Blended learning

This is a new trend of learning, which has brought in a major transformation in teaching-learning scenario because it combines face to face classroom learning with online learning (collaborative interaction between the learners and faculty through the web). It provides maximum opportunities students to interact online in the class thus providing a more flexible schedule. Blended or hybrid learning provides option for students to learn online as well as in class. Thus, there consist of a mixture of face to face learning and online learning. E.g. – teleconferencing, social software in academia, LCD projectors etc.

Digital Learning

Digital learning with quality contents, animation, and interactive chart are becoming popular in the students. Digital learning is becoming norm for many courses like Library and information science, Management, Digital marketing etc.

Personalized Learning

Education systems are increasingly investigating the use of technology to better understand a student's knowledge base from prior learning and to tailor teaching to both address learning gaps as well as learning styles. This focus transforms a classroom from one that teaches to the middle to one that adjusts content and pedagogy based on individual student needs both strong and weak.

CERTAIN CRITERIA REQUIRED FOR ICT IN EDUCATION

Infrastructure : For enhancing education, through ICT, the most important of all is ICT infrastructure i.e. appropriate buildings, rooms, furniture.

English language : In the globalized era English has emerged as the dominant language of the internet. An estimated of 80% of the online courses are in English. Software produced in the world market is in English.

Trained teachers in ICT age : Most of the teachers in India lack ICT skills thereby affecting the quality. Large number of teachers lack ICT skills. Very few have idea about research basing on ICT.

Therefore, ICT is of immense importance to bring the gap between knowledge and quality. ICT has now become increasingly affordable, accessible and interactive. It can reach people in remote areas so as to expose them to education, it can improve classroom teaching. And change people's mind set towards education.

OTHER EMERGING TRENDS IN HIGHER EDUCATION

Lifelong learning

Lifelong education in a modern and wider sense is a concept that emphasizes on providing education to all with the help of non-formal and in-formal educational agencies. There is no age bar. The most spectacular benefit is that one can learn at his own pace, time and convenience.

Cloud Computing

Applications are increasingly moving off of the stand alone desk top computer and increasingly onto server farms accessible through the Internet. The implications of this trend for education systems are huge; they will make cheaper information appliances available which do not require the processing power or size of the PC. The challenge will be providing the ubiquitous connectivity to access information sitting in the "cloud".

DIGITAL LIBRARY

INFLIBNET: This is basically an interconnection of libraries throughout the world. The information and library network (INFLIBNET) centre was established in May 1996 as an independent autonomous inter university centre of the UGC (university grants commission). It includes automation of academic libraries and information centres, promote resource sharing among academic libraries. The programmes of the INFLIBNET centre include copy cataloguing, internet connectivity under UGC INFONET and others.

CO-OPERATIVE LEARNING

This is a new concept in learning; it is an instructional use of small groups so that students work together to maximize their own and each other's learning. Co-operative learning must be structured to include the essential elements, like positive inter-pendency, face to face interaction, group skills, group processing, and accountability.

Co-operative learning ensures: The mastery of the content, retention of material, generation of new ideas, and transfer of learning, reasoning strategies.

Is essential that –

The group is heterogeneous Equal opportunity is given.

Access to learning

Provide sufficient time

Recognition and reward

Encourage co-operative thinking.

3G-MOBILE LEARNING

3G-Mobile learning is the outcome of wireless technology which has spread widely in information and technology world. Mobile learning has also added to the tremendous impact to teaching-learning and student collaboration. It has decreased the limitation of learning location. The 3G-system allows simultaneous use of speech and data device, mobile internet access, video calls, mobile TV.

It is a fact that mobile phone technology has faster access to the web world. The 3G mobile learning has lately emerged to be associated with fast connectivity to education. It paves a way for the launch of 3rd generation users to enable them to access internet and download videos, voice files and advanced information related to education at a much faster pace.

CONCLUSION

Therefore, LIS education is acknowledged as crucial elements for imparting know ledged based education.

Innovation is seen as a major source of modern productive growth. Universities prepare effective workforce for the country who are technologically advanced, more productive and has led to tremendous growth of human skills, which create mechanisms for knowledge transfer, innovations, intra and inter knowledge integration, local capacity building etc. New trends are emerging everyday so as to cater to the needs of the new generation of students and create employability.

REFERENCES

- Sharma & Sharma (2006) Educational technology and management; New Delhi: Krishna Publishers
- University News-Vol:29; No-12;2011
- University News-Vol:49; No-6;2011
- University News-Vol:49; No-10;2011
- Malhan, I. V. (2009), "Exploring the opportunities in the emerging information environment for transformation of LIS education", *ibid.* pp. 57-65.
- Stephen, A. (2008) "Libraries and the global technological forecast", *Delnet Newsletter,* Vol. 15 No.1&2, pp.15-19.
- Wijetunge, P. (2009) "Selection of students to LIS education programmes in Sri Lanka and some related issues", in Envisioning employable LIS courses in developing countries for the emerging knowledge society 2009 papers of the xxvi national conference in Burdwan, India, 2009, IATLIS, Patiala, pp. 66-77.
- Velmurugan.C. (2010). Challenges and lingering issues of library and information science education through digital environment, presented at IATLIS 2010, XXVII National conference, p.350-354.
- Chandrashekara M and Ramasesh C. P(2009) Library and information science research in India, Asia –pacific conference on library & information education & practice, pp-530-537.
- Mahapatra, G. (2006). LIS education in India: Emerging paradigms, challenges and propositions in the digital era. Presented at the Asia-Pacific Conference on Library & Information Education & Practice, 2006 (A-LIEP 2006), Singapore, 3-6 April 2006.

16
Library and Information Science Education : Options, Opportunities and Future

Sujeeta Soni
Jyoti Singh
Shahbeena Begum
M. Phil. I.Sc. IInd Semester,
Thakur Ranmat Singh Autonomous
College Rewa (M.P.)

INTRODUCTION

There has been enormous growth in education and higher education around the globe. Every country worth its name has developed a system of education and infrastructure to educate its people, and India is no exception. There has been a fast growth in institution of higher education since the dawn of twentieth century and more particularly, after India attained independence in 1947. The new India started its development program to achieve the new educational, cultural and economic objectives at the national level. Such developments at these institutions contributed to the development of more libraries, which in turn had to accept new responsibilities to meet society's changing needs and demands. Libraries are recognized to play an important role in education, scientific research and social-economic development of a country. This envisages the need for professionally qualified personnel to manage and run the libraries and information centers effectively and efficiently. In order to feed the growing number of libraries, more trained library professionals were needed. For this purpose, library science departments started springing up, and library science developed into a distinct field of specialization with its own normative principles, theories, techniques, and practices that were deemed sufficient to meet the growing dimensions of library services.

Handling of recorded knowledge in modern libraries has given birth to the functional aspects of collecting, organizing and promoting the use of reading materials relevant to the users through information transfer activities. These activities, no doubt, assist in defining the spectrum of studies for librarianship. The basic tenet of LIS education is to provide balanced training, integrating theory with practical exercises, and to cover all aspects of professional work with equal emphasis embracing new frontier of librarianship. LIS education aims at providing trained manpower to manage different types of libraries, information and documentation centers which, over a period of time have undergone changes in terms of needs, functions, types and range of services offered as well as tools and techniques being used when offering the services. Research in library and information science in India is not deep rooted. In the beginning it was in the form of a trail and error method. It was Padamashee S R Ranganathan (1889-1972) who lifted librarianship to the level of a science with the formulation of laws of library science, and establishment library schools and research centers. He even graded them as normative principles, fundamental laws, canons, principles and postulates . Ranganathan cut new grounds and blazed new trails in library and information science initially by solo research. This is evidence from the published literature that Ranganathan era's is characterized by a period of intellectual contribution to the library and information science, particularly library classification. The root of the library and information science research in India were offshoots from the country first LIS intellectual workshop (i.e., Department of Library and Information Science, University of Delhi) instituted by the Dr SR Ranganathan a doyen of library science profession in India in 1946. And the first research fruit in the library and information science in the country even in the commonwealth countries was awarded by the University of Delhi in 1957 to the DB Krishna Rao for his thesis 'Facet Analysis and Depth Classification of Agriculture' under the supervision of Dr. SR Ranganathan.

HISTORICAL DEVELOPMENT

The modern period in the history of education for librarianship began in the mid-1800s as librarians around the world recognized that systematic education and training were required so that order could be brought to the collections that had been growing in all libraries. The need for professionally qualified personnel to manage and run these libraries effectively and efficiently was duly recognized during the first half of the present and consequently, the library education programme had been started at several places much before Independence. The history of the education of library science in India may be traced far back as the year of 1911 with the starting of a short term training programme in library science in the Baroda State, under the patronage of Maharaj Sayajirao Gaekwar of Baaroda, who, impressed by the splendid work done by public libraries in the West, secured the services of an American librarian Mr. W. A. Borden as Director of the State Library Department. Mr. Bordon had been a pupil of Mr. Melvil Dewey, who established the first library school in the Columbia

College, New York in 1887. In 1915, another student of Dewey, Mr. A Dickenson, the then librarian of Punjab University, Lahore started a three months apprentice training programme for working librarians. Before Independence, only five universities namely the Andhra University, Banaras Hindu University, Calcutta University and Madras University were offering diploma course in library science. Library education was given a new status and design by Professor S. R. Ranganathan in 1920, when the first systematic programme in library education was started under the auspices of the Madras Library Association in collaboration with the Madras University. This library school was subsequently taken over by the Madras University in 1931 and in 1937 the course was converted into Postgraduate (PG) Diploma in Library Science. This was the first diploma programme in Library Science in India. University of Delhi was the first university to establish a full-fledged Department of Library Science just before independence in 1946, and started admitting students to the PG Diploma in 1947. In 1951, the diploma was changed to Master in Library Science (M.Lib.Sc). Later, between 1956 to 1959, six new LIS departments were established at Aligarh Muslim University, M.S.University of Baroda, Nagpur University, Osmania University, Pune University and Vikram University. Since 1960s, the number of LIS departments has continued to increase.

After Independence the stimulus for the growth and development of libraries and library science education has come from the progress in and extension of education, scientific research and programmes of socio-economic development which started in 1951 with the commencement of the First Five-Year Plan. As a result of these developments, Library and Information Science today is a well-recognized discipline of study and research at the post-graduate level in more than hundred universities in the country. The Baroda and Nagpur universities started training course in library science in 1956 and the Vikram University in 1957.

PRESENT STATUS OF LIS EDUCATION IN INDIA

Since its inception decades ago, LIS education has grown and developed into a full-fledged multi-disciplinary subject. LIS courses at bachelors, masters and research level are being imparted by different institutions – university departments, colleges, library associations and specialized institutions. There are now 96 universities in India imparting Library and Information Science education as independent departments in different levels. The list is shown in Table . Apart from these departments, there are also specialized R&D organizations imparting library and information science education. Worth mentioning is the two years Associateship in Documentation and Information Science (ADIS) imparted by Documentation Research & Training Institute (DRTC), Indian Statistical Institute, Bangalore (Karnataka) and National Institute of Science Communication And Information Resources (NISCAIR) formerly INSDOC, New Delhi which is equivalent to Mater degree of Library & Information Science (LIS). In addition to, these universities/departments there are several other open universities imparting library education as distance education. The professional associations such as Delhi Library Association (DLA) and the polytechnic institutions throughout the country are also imparting LIS education as lower level such as Certificate/Diploma in Library & Information Science.

With the realization of the importance of higher education and research, research in Library education is not lagging behind like other disciplines. The University Grants Commission (UGC) and the Indian Council of Social Science Research (ICSSR) are promoting research in library and information science by awarding scholarships to doctoral students.

OBJECTIVES OF LIBRARY AND INFORMATION SCIENCE EDUCATION

The goal of library and information science education is the preparation of personnel for the task of successful performance at different levels of competence in different types of libraries with an insight into the role of these libraries in a fast changing society. It should impart a thorough grounding in the intellectual foundations of the profession and competence in the technical and technological skills required for their day-to-day practice in different positions. In other words, education for library and information science should be both knowledge and theory oriented task or practice oriented. The two aspects of theory and practice should blend harmoniously in a sound programme of library and information science education because on this will depend the effectiveness and success of the programme. In achieving this objective the methods of teaching and evaluation employed are as important as the quality of the faculty.

The main objectives of LIS profession are to: provide training for building up leadership qualities among the LIS profession; develop knowledge on the latest techniques of information storage, transfer and retrieval; help to acquire necessary skills in handling, accessing and application of electronic resources, tools and media; and help to know the latest developments in the Information Technology (IT)

To sum up, the basic aims of library and information science education may be as follows

- To develop necessary technical skills;
- To develop administrative skills;
- To develop service orientation;
- To develop thorough knowledge of various sources of information, necessary to give the traditional and modern library services;

- To develop professional awareness.

LEVELS OF EDUCATION

Out of the 96 university departments, 56 departments conduct the one-year Bachelors degree and one year Masters degree in Library and Information Science at the postgraduate level. Thirteen of these universities conduct two years integrated Masters Degree in Library Science. These programme further leads to M.Phil. and Ph.D. levels. The levels of LIS education in India are discussed as follows:

Certificate/Diploma in Library Science (C/D.Lib. Sc.)

Many polytechnic colleges, schools and Library Associations impart the low level of library science courses in India having duration of six months to one year. The basic qualification for these courses is 10+2. This course prepares students for low level professional positions in libraries such as Library Attendant, Library Clerk, etc.

Bachelor of Library and Information Science (BLIS)

This is a one-year post graduate degree course. The basic eligibility is a three years degree from any discipline. This course prepares students for junior professional positions.

Master of Library and Information Science (MLIS)

Master of Library and Information Science is imparted as a one-year post graduate degree course in some universities while in some, it is conducted as a two years integrated course. Many universities which offered one year BLISc and MLISc courses are now switching to two years integrated MLIS course in the line of other maters degree courses. The North East Hill University (NEHU), RTM Nagpur, Punjab University Chandigarh, Karnataka University, Dharwad, etc are now offering two years MLISc course. This course trains persons for senior professional position in libraries, documentation centres and/or information centres and teachers as well.

Associateship in Documentation and Information Science (ADIS)

The Documentation Research and Training Centre (DRTC), Bangalore (Karnataka) offers two years Associateship in Documentation and Information Science (Now know as Master of Science in Information Science). The National Institute of Science Communication And Information Resources (NISCAIR), New Delhi , formerly INSDOC also impart two years documentation programme i.e., Associateship in Documentation (AID) after graduation. The course offered by the DRTC and NISCAIR have upper age on the courses as offered by the universities departments in terms of ICT syllabus and intake of the enrolments.

MASTER OF PHILOSOPHY IN LIBRARY AND INFORMATION SCIENCE

M.Phil. in Library and Information Science prepares a student for further advanced research in LIS. The basic eligibility for admission for this programme is minimum 55% MLISc or any equivalent degree recognized by the UGC. With candidates having more qualifications are being preferred for superior position, many students are opting for M.Phil. Courses to better equip them for better positions.

DOCTOR OF PHILOSOPHY OF LIBRARY AND INFORMATION SCIENCE

This is an advanced level of research programme being offered after the completion of MLISc or M.Phil. Degree depending on the universities. The general aim of a research degree, whether M.Phil. or Ph.D. is to provide training in doing research as well as to develop in the candidate a critical and analytical process of thinking with the purpose that they would be able to provide leadership in the profession. They would also be able to help librarians and information scientists to develop techniques and skills required to meet their requirements of the fast changing society. They should be able to identify the needs, set objectives, identify and analyze the problems and find appropriate solutions. They would also be in a position to participate in the planning, organization and implementation of programmes at various levels.

ROLE OF UNIVERSITY OF DELHI IN LIS EDUCATION

The Department of Library and information Science instituted in 1946 under the Faculty of Arts by the two eminent library science scholars namely Padamashree (late) Dr. S.R. Ranganathan (1892-1972), National Research Professor (1965-1972) in library science and the (late) Prof. S. Das Gupta (1912-1966) the first Delhi University Librarian and Professor Head Department of Library and Information Science, University of Delhi.

The Department has credit to become the first LIS Department in country to impart quality LIS education & research through various levels i.e. BLISc (earlier known as D.Lib. Sc and B.Lib. Sc.), M.L.I.Sc (1956), M. Phil (1976), and Ph.D (1957). It was the first LIS School, which constituted at par with the other teaching departments in this University. The 1996-97 year was celebrated as 'Golden Jubilee Year' by organizing a national seminar on 'National Seminar on the Need Based Innovative Programmme for Education and Training of LIS Personnel' which was attended more than 160 participants of Delhi and adjoining states since than such activities are the common in the Department. The Department has also been recognized as an Associated Project of UNESCO. It is housed in the Tutorial Building, Second Floor, adjacent to the University Central Library.

The root of the library and information science (LIS) research in India has been sprouted /offshoots from the country first LIS Department .The Department during the past 64 years of its existence has played a significant role in the LIS research and education in the country.

Already about 3256 students have taken their Library Science degree from this Department. Out of whom about 2069 students obtained Postgraduate Diploma in Library Science/ Bachelor's degree in Library Science; 1000 Master's degree in Library Science / Master's Degree in Library and Information Science; 90 M. Phil. Degree and 50 Ph.D degrees in Library and Information Science. Old students are occupying senior professional positions not only in India but also outside the country.

OUTLINE THE COURSES AND PROGRAMMES

The department has many credits in the context of LIS education and research in India. From the above section we can understand that it is the first Department of the country to initiate/start first formal education and research in LIS almost at all the levels in the country. To pace with the development and new trends, to meet the supply and demand of the LIS professionals the Department regularly revised and updated their syllabi. The first revision was took place in 1970 with the introduction of a paper namely computer application in libraries (for the first time in country) and many optional papers at Master's level to accommodate the more specialized papers in the various sub-fields of LIS. The revised syllabi has a beautiful provision or flexibility to the faculty to include new emerged concepts in their concerned subject in order to make the syllabi more updated. The second revision was took place in 2004, after a long gap almost 32 years. The syllabi-2004 also incorporate all significant contents as proposed in the 'UGC model curriculum, Library and Information Science' recommended by the UGC for implementation in all LIS schools in India. Very recently the Department for the third time thoroughly re-revised and re-restructured the syllabi of BLIS and MLIS, which can be considered one of the best syllabi in the country. The brief outline of revised syllabi for BLIS and MLIS (2009) are as:-

BACHELOR OF LIBRARY & INFORMATION SCIENCE (BLIS)

First Semester

B-101 Library, Information and Society

B-102 Library Classification (Theory)

B-103 Library Classification (Practical)

B-104 Basics of Information Technology in LIS (Theory)

B-105 Basics of Information Technology in LIS (Practical)

B-106 Project Work in LIS: (a) Literature Survey (b) Field Survey

Second Semester

B-107 Management of Library and Information Centres

B-108 Information Sources and Services

B-109 Library Cataloguing (Theory)

B-110 Library Cataloguing (Practical)

B-111 Internship Programme
(a) Report on Training Activities
(b) Viva-Voce (Based on Internship Training)

MATER OF LIBRARY & INFORMATION SCIENCE (MLIS)

First Semester

M-101 Information Systems and Programmes

M-102 Advanced Knowledge Organisations: Classification (Practical)

M-103 Advanced Knowledge Organisation: Cataloguing (Practical)

M-104 Information and Communication Technology Applications in LIS (Theory)

M-105 Research Methodology

M-106 Marketing of Library and Information Products and Services

Second Semester

M-107 Information and Communication Technology Applications in LIS (Practical)

M-108 Information Storage and Retrieval System

M-109 Information Literacy Applications in LIS

M-110 Elective Papers

M-110 (a) Public Library and Information System

M-110 (b) Academic Library and Information System

M-110 (c) Research and Technical Library and Information System

M-110 (d) Health Science Library and Information System

M-110 (e) Agricultural Sciences Library Information System

M-110 (f) Engineering and Technological Library and Information System

M 111 Elective Interdisciplinary PapersM-111 (a) Print and Electronic Sources and Literature in Humanities

M-111 (b) Print and Electronic Sources and Literature in Natural Sciences

M-111 (c) Print and Electronic Sources and Literature in Social Science

M-112 Project Work: (a) Project Report (b) Viva-Voce

JOB OPPORTUNITIES AND PLACES

The position of libraries globally at par with the temples in the Hindu home families, means libraries are found almost in all institutions or organizations irrespective their nature and types. In modern times the libraries became the integral part of their originations or institutions. To run the temples and other ritual entities we need the priest or pujari similarly to run the libraries we need the library professionals to serve the various kinds of users. The organizations such as DRDO, CSIR, ISRO, NAL, HAL, ICAR, ICMR, BARC, AICTE, etc need the highly qualified LIS professionals to manage their information centers. Due the advent of ICT and its application in libraries new options and opportunities emerged.

The library workers today's known by the various designations form traditional such as (Librarian, Reference Librarian, Documentation Officer, and Information Officer) to Information Scientists, Technical Officer, Scientific Officer, Knowledge Manager, Resource Manager, Chief Knowledge Officer, etc. In nutshell, in the LIS profession there are abundant job opportunities.

17

Trends, Challenges and Future of Library and Information Science Education

Sujeeta Soni
M. Phil. I.Sc. IInd Semester, Thakur Ranmat Singh Autonomous College Rewa (M.P.)

INTRODUCTION

Library and information science education in India is largely a 20th century phenomenon. It has a history of a century behind it and has developed into a distinct discipline to meet the growing dimensions of library service and the changing needs of the society. Realising the importance of professionally trained personnel to manage libraries effectively and efficiently, library training programmes were started at several places even before independence. The first formal course for librarianship training in India was started sometime in 1911 in Baroda1.

LIS education is linked with the growth of libraries. The origin and growth of the libraries depend on the educational and culturaln conditions of the society at any time2. Library as a social organ has certain social obligations. These obligations vary with the educational and cultural needs. The personnel working in libraries must have proper library education then only they can use and implement the library techniques effectively to suit the requirements of the users. The LIS professionals should take responsibility to educate the users in accessing required information and must keep them update to cope up with the ever-changing information requirements3.

LIS EDUCATION IN INDIA : AN OVERVEW

The origin of librarianship, the temporal changes in its discourse and delivery provides a metamorphosis of the influence of several factors. For instance, the library education commenced with training till a formal course in library science was started in the US by Melvil Dewey. Today, study of knowledge management and knowledge organisation inherently stands on the edifice built by him. Training and education in LIS in India dates back to 1911 and has kept pace with the developed countries of the world. It is gradually evolving and has spread its roots throughout the country. The credit for starting a formal course in library education in India goes to William Alonson Borden and Asa Don Dickinson, both students of Melvil Dewey. Alonson Borden started a training course in 1911 at the Central Library, Baroda, followed by Dickinson in 1915 at the Punjab University, Lahore (now in Pakistan). Thereafter, other universities and library associations also started setting up library schools.

Madras Library Association in 1928, and Bengal Library Association in 1935 started a certificate course for librarians. Among the universities, Madras University under the leadership of Dr S.R. Ranganathan, took over the certificate course from Madras Library Association in 1931, and later in 1937, converted the course into a Postgraduate Diploma in Library Science. It was the first diploma course in library science in India. The Andhra University in 1935, Banaras Hindu University in 1941, and the University of Delhi in 1947 are some other universities which started this course. The University of Delhi in 1948, under the guidance of Dr Ranganathan, started a Master's degree course in library science and also provided facilities for research leading to PhD. It was the first university to start the MPhil course in 1977.

Presently, library education is being provided by a variety of institutions such as traditional universities, open universities, deemed universities, polytechnics, affiliated colleges, professional associations, and documentation centres, etc. Currently, there are about 120 universities, including correspondence and open universities, in India offering LIS education at Bachelor's and Master's levels, and 63 universities which offer doctoral degree in library science. Besides, National Institute of Science Communication and Information Resources (NISCAIR), New Delhi, and Documentation Research and Training Centre, Bangalore, offer two-year Associateship in Information Science. The LIS education has expanded vertically, but there are marked disparities in its profile, curriculum, available infrastructure, and in the levels of collaboration. The condition of LIS education in many developing countries is also the same.

TRENDS IN LIS EDUCATION IN INDIA

Common trends noted in the growth of LIS schools around the world are review and revision of curricula, increased use of ICT, decrease or increase in the number of students, amalgamation and reorientation. These trends noted in the context of Indian LIS programmes are relocation of the academic administration of LIS schools (Information Science at the University of Madras, and NISCAIR in New Delhi), and expansion of LIS departments.

LEVELS OF LIS EDUCATION

Changes that took place in India in the field of LIS from the initial stages to the present day can be identified as informal training to formal training; certificate to diploma; diploma to degree; and degree to research programme. Further, changes in the curriculum of these courses have taken place in response to the changing conditions and demands. At Master's level, special courses such as computer applications, system analysis, industrial information and medical information systems, expert systems, knowledge management, economics of information, marketing of information, digital libraries, etc., have also been introduced.

LIS EDUCATION IN INDIAN LANGUAGES

The medium of instruction plays a vital role in imparting education, particularly professional education. Language is a vehicle to transmit knowledge and the library professionals exist to facilitate communication. It is an unsolved debate whether to impart LIS education in English or in regional languages.Though many schools are teaching LIS in English, but allowing students to write their examinations in their mother tongue.

There are certain implications in imparting LIS education in regional languages. These are: availability of expertise, curriculum, and course material; background of students seeking LIS education; marketability of LIS graduates and postgraduates who have studied in regional languages; national integrity; trends in LIS education at international level and global village concept. Hence, LIS education in India would be much more effective if imparted in English only. Further, imparting LIS education in regional languages may impede the very philosophy of the subject. Still teaching at Certificate and Bachelor's levels in regional languages is dominating in some Indian library schools.

DISTANCE EDUCATION OF LIS IN INDIA

Distance education (DE) in India has its roots in the early 1960s. It was mainly confined to the courses in arts, social sciences and humanities at graduate and postgraduate levels. The first open university (Andhra Pradesh Open University, now Dr B.R. Ambedkar Open University) in India was established at Hyderabad. This was followed by Indira Gandhi National Open University (IGNOU) in 1985 on the lines of the British Open University. The DE in LIS was started in the early 1980s by Dr B.R. Ambedkar Open University (the then Andhra Pradesh Open University) and Annamalai University. Since then, there is a phenomenal increase and growth of the learners through DE. The number of DE institutions has also increased considerably due to economic viability and as a means of additional resource generation for the parent universities. A list of universities offering LIS courses in India through DE is given in Table.

LIS EDUCATION IN INDIA: ISSUES AND CHALLENGES

The policy makers of LIS education in India including University Grants Commission, Ministry of Human Resource Development, National Assessment and Accreditation Council, Experts Committee Members of LIS, teaching community and management should take into account the following issues/challenges at the national level and a uniform policy for all the academic institutions in the country for the development of LIS profession towards better recognition at par with any other discipline.

FUTURE OF LIS EDUCATION IN INDIA

A broad perspective of LIS education in the developing and developed nations gives an indication that LIS education in India needs to enhance some of the vital aspects such as large scale integration of the allied subject fields. Harmonisation of teachinglearning programmes, collaboration and exchange, use of the facilities offered by international and global organisations and induction of the equity components are absolutely must to get recognition in the national and international job market.

These days, the concept of assessment and accreditation has taken roots in the higher education system. Establishment of few model schools of LIS education on the pattern of Royal School of LIS, Denmark, will encourage and enrich the quality of LIS education to suit the multiple requirements of employers in the job market. This may also further the value of LIS education, which can greatly contribute to the R&D, and development of cultural and corporate sectors including the service sector17.

In view of this, it is desirable that the library schools in India must adapt themselves to the changing situations so that they can turnout better professionals who can meet the challenges posed by the changing environment. Library schools that are not able to adapt themselves may become irrelevant and have to close down sooner or later in the years to come. History has a lesson to teach. In the USA, those library schools which did not moved with the time, were either closed or merged with other schools dealing with information science/information studies.

CONCLUSION

Today, LIS education is no more an education for the mangers of libraries only, but has become an education for the consumers of knowledge also. It is a change from managing libraries by librarians to manage the flow of information by one and all. Earlier, LIS students after the education became librarians, now professionals teach this science and learners choose this profession to manage theinformation.

The need of mere library schools is over in the present context. Better schools having adequate finance, physical and library facilities, equipment, and qualified and experienced faculty is the need of the hour. The LIS schools should aim at educational excellence and serve as pacesetters. Such schools should try to produce a new breed of professionals capable to successfully perform their role in the fast changing information needs of the society using new information technologies such as word processors, dedicated special purpose microcomputers, and telecommunication technology. The library schools should assume the role of leadership and responsibility to produce competent manpower for the present as well as future needs of different kinds of information centres including university libraries. To conclude in the words of Lancaster: "We must shift the focus of our professional concern away from the Library as an institution and towards the skilled professionals who will become a professional practitioner on par with medical and legal practitioners."

It is often said that the 'future is uncertain', but the future of LIS professionals can be visualised now itself unless and until necessary measures are taken by the LIS teachers in particular to train the forthcoming incumbents with the most up-to-date curriculum emphasising more on ICT skills so as to prepare the information professionals for leadership role. Mere blaming the librarians is not a solution to the visibility of librarianship, but at the same time, a unique accreditation or certification system, quality of education and distance education trend has to be monitored.

18

Community Reading Room (Public Library) as an Instrument in Eradication of Adult Illiteracy: A Case Study of Eritrea (North East Africa)

Yogesh Bajpai

Assistant Professor, Department of Library and Information Science, College of Natural and Computational Sciences, Mekelle University, Mekelle, P.O.Box-231, Ethiopia

ABSTRACT

Community reading rooms (CRRs) are an extension of Eritrea's Public Library Service into rural areas for adult literacy programs. At its beginning in 1993, the CRR project was closely linked to the adult literacy programme of the Department of Adult Education of Eritrea. The CRRs were intended primarily to serve adult literacy learners and newly literate adults. However, because the CRRs had to be housed at first in existing school buildings, farmers, schoolchildren have become the most active and most numerous users. The villages have claimed the CRRs as an important part of community life.

Key Words : Rural Libraries, Community Reading Rooms, Eritrea

INTRODUCTION

The Community Reading Rooms project in Eritrea serves as an outreach service for communities far away from the major centres where public libraries are not located. In Eritrea still they have not established Eritrean National Library and National Library Service outreach programmes include the Mobile Libraries and the Book Box Service. These days there are approximately 83 community reading rooms are serving for rural Eritrean society, 15 Community Reading Rooms were first piloted in 1993.

Community reading rooms (rural libraries) are important features of the literacy programme especially in the rural areas. They are important sources of information for the learners and as such are expected to cultivate reading habits among the rural people. However, their coverage is limited, as they are only about 83 nationwide (Ministry of Education, 2011). Also, they currently possess very limited reading materials in science, social science, and language, particularly in mother tongue. Most contain available in Tigrinya, and only a few feature materials in Tigre and Bilen (the Adult Education Department is trying to publish reading material in other 5 Eritrean ethnic languages). The attendants or para-librarian have not received any relevant adequate training. By broadcasting educational topics such as health, environment, social, legal and agricultural issues etc. in 4 local languages for the public and the illiterate population in particular through the educational radio program of the Ministry of Education. All these effort is to cerate literate environment and to sustain learning and promote life long learning.

The Community Reading Rooms (CRRs) are a rural library network originally aimed at providing basic reading material to neoliterates who have gone through the Department of Adult Literacy (DAL) Programme. The service is similar to that of the public library, but on a very small scale. Each CRR starts with a base stock of 250 titles. There is a reference section, a periodicals section that may only be used on the premises, and the normal circulation service. Users may borrow one book at a time for a period of one week. The CRRs are also serving as social/cultural centres. In most villages, the CRR is the only building with electricity; so many cultural and social activities take place there.

SCOPE OF THE STUDY

Eritrea is one of the countries that have the highest share of the world's illiterate population. At this stage, about 70 percent of the country's adult population is illiterate. Despite Eritrea's commitment and determination to provide basic education for all, 66.6 percent children are currently out of the school system, these are potential adult illiterates. These high rates, combined with the persisting gender and regional disparities in education, are totally intolerable social situation in a country such as Eritrea where human capacity development is the top priority.

OBJECTIVE OF THE STUDY

- To introduce and execute theoretical concept of Community Reading Room (rural public library) to enhance adult literacy rates/ programmes.
- To design adult literary campaign for the benefit of different segments of Eritrean society, especially with the help of CRRs.
- To educate people with emerging audio-visual aids to enhance literacy rate amongst them.
- To measure and quantify the impact of adult literacy campaign in Eritrea and suggest prospective strategies to enhance its productivity/efficacy.

HYPOTHESES

Eritrea was affected by famine, draft and war, due to these reasons adult illiteracy is highest in this country. If the Ministry of Education of Eritrea and the Department of adult literacy of Eritrea provide good reading environment like public libraries (community reading rooms) to these people, it will be the effective medium for the growth of the adult literacy. Rural libraries have been played vital role in Botswana, Kenya, and Tanzania in eradication of adult literacy. CRRs for this country definitely will make a positive, vital change in literacy, economic and social growth.

THE BLUEPRINT OF THE CRR IN AFRICAN NATIONS

The idea of Community Reading Rooms was first mooted in Africa at the Botswana Library Association's (BLA) Libraries and Literacy Conference held in Kanye, a southern rural village in Botswana, in 1985. The idea was born out of a perceived need to take library services to the grassroots. The BLA Kanye Conference brought together librarians and literacy personnel to develop a common strategy that could offer the illiterate population the means to become functionally literate. It also was a move to promote maximum use of the Public Library Service. It was fueled by the vision behind the work of the Department of Adult Education (DAE). The DAE is the department in the Ministry of Education with responsibility for adult literacy. The DAE had realized that although it could provide literacy skills to its adult literacy pupils, there would have to be a grassroots library service to sustain these basic literacy skills. In the development of the CRR project, the DAE worked hand-in-hand with the Department of National Library Service. (Margaret Baffour-Awuah, 2001)

THE CRR STRUCTURES

One of the issues that needed to be immediately

resolved was where the CRRs could be established? It was not practicable to build structures immediately. That would take time. So it was agreed that, to begin with, they would be housed in the primary schools. Most of the rural primary schools have no electricity, and the CRRs are meant to be used every day after school is over. Therefore, a large classroom was to be selected and provided with solar-panel electricity by the Eritrean Electricity Service. The electrification was funded by the Swedish International Development Agency (SIDA). (For many years, SIDA supported developmental programmes of the Adult Literacy in Eritrea, during the year of 1998-2002 GOE and SIDA funded 2830014.33 U S Dollars).

STAFFING THE CRRS: LITERACY GROUP LEADERS

The question of who was to run the Village Reading Rooms and what sort of qualifications were necessary, was answered with the cooperation of DAE. Their Literacy Group Leaders would run the CRRs on a part-time basis. The rationale here was that if the Literacy Group Leaders were also running the CRRs, they could guide the adult literacy pupils on choice of material related to their studies and interests better than anybody else. The concept of the barefoot librarian was raised at the Standing Conference of Eastern, Central and Southern African Librarians in 1986. The term *barefoot librarian* meant an untrained community person with basic literacy skills who could be trained on the job. Because she or he would be from the community and would have been involved with literacy teaching, such a person would have a much better understanding of the needs of the adult learners than anybody else could have needs in terms of necessary life skills, and needs in terms of reading and numeracy skills.

When the Village Reading Room project was started, the DAE agreed that the Literacy Group Leaders who were employed and paid honoraria by the DAE would also be paid by the MoE to work as' assistant and supervise the Village Reading Rooms. Most of the learners in the literacy project were continually on the move between the villages where they normally live, their lands where their farms 83 Rural Libraries (CRR) were, and the cattle posts where the animals were herded. This mobility meant that the Literacy Group Leaders could never correctly predict how busy they would be, and the class sizes were fluid. The Literacy Group Leaders, therefore, had the time both to run the CRRs and to monitor the progress of their adult pupils. It also meant that they could receive double honoraria from both the Departments.

PREVIOUS LITERACY PROJECTS IN ERITREA

During the armed struggle for independence (1961-1991) literacy training was conducted among the freedom fighters (that was the first concept of community reading room in Eritrea). The training was considered a comprehensive success because of the high increase of literacy. And it was accepted as an important instrument for the political consciousness, unity and effective participation towards the goal of total independence. Literacy training work was not limited to the fighters only. It was also provided to the Eritrean communities in the librated areas. Although the effort was frequently interrupted by war and successive drought, it was useful in many ways. The commitment of the organizers and teachers, the fraternal relationship developed among learners and teachers, innovations and flexibilities experienced to overcome constrains and challenges and others were some of the legacies that can be highlighted. Despite the possible contextual difference between now and then, there are several lessons that can be drawn in the areas of organization of learners (class organization), flexibility in setting out learning hours, provision of functional knowledge and skills in relation to the literacy training and target clienteles.

After the independence (1991) small scale literacy projects were trialled in some parts of the country. These were initiated by different agencies. The major providers of the literacy projects in the years between 1992 and 1997 were the National Union of Eritrean Women (NUEW) and the Ministry of Education (MOE). Donor agencies, who participated in developing and funding adult literacy projects, implemented by ministry of education included UNICEF, WVI, UNDP, and UNESCO.

The main objective of these projects was to provide basic literacy and numeracy skills alongwith knowledge in some functional subjects such as hygiene, civics, and environmental issues to adult illiterates. Duplication of activities and dispersion of efforts were strongly felt during the past seventeen year's experience, calling for more efficient and effective coordination.

FIRST AND SECOND LITERACY PROJECTS 1993-1998

The first literacy project, (1993-1995) focused on the remote rural areas of the country to reach out to the disadvantaged. This project faced many constraints, which stemmed form improper planning and monitoring producers. Basically it lacked on essential feasibility assessment from the outset in identifying the potential learners, availability of convenient learning sites and supervision mechanisms. As a consequence, the number of participants and centres declined drastically. The life span of the projects was three years, but 18 out of the 25 centres phased out earlier. Had an assessment and situational analysis been done, major constraints and attitudes towards the literacy project would have been noted and actions taken accordingly (Aimut, T, 2001)

In 1994/95 another literacy project was initiated in collaboration with World Vision Eritrea (WVE). This project was different form previous ones in that all of the participants were women affiliated to the same ethnic group speaking the same language. For the convenience of monitoring and follow up, the sites chosen were villages in the highlands for from the main roads. Initially the projects started with 4 canters and increased to 16 in the following year. This further expended to more than 190 canters when UNDP joined the effort. Childcare enter services were also attached to each literacy canter to help mothers concentrate on the literacy work. This was highly accepted by the concerned mother and the community.

Literacy enrolment, dropout and completion by year and Gender (1993-1998)

	Gender	Years					
		1993/ 94	**1994/ 95**	**1995/ 96**	**1996/ 97**	**1997/ 98**	**Total**
Enrolled	Male	2494	869	648	331	655	4997
	Female	1447	1268	6929	5816	10922	26382
	Total	3941	2137	7577	6147	11577	31379
Drop-out	Male	1651	461	433	184	330	2059
	Female	949	544	2095	1253	3311	8152
	Total	2600	1005	2528	1437	3641	11211
Completed	Male	883	410	203	147	355	1998
	Female	418	722	4838	4563	7581	18123
	Total	1301	1132	5042	4710	7936	20121
%Comp-	Male	35	47	31	44	54	40
leted	Female	29	57	70	78	69	69
	Total	33	53	67	61	68	64
Centers		25	19	100	98	193	435
Facilitators		138	78	272	214	432	1134

Source: Essential Statistical Indicators MOE 1998/99

Table 1 shows that the majority of the participants in the literacy projects conducted in the past six years (1993-1998) were women (84%). Another important trend shown in the table is that completion rates increased from 33 percents in the 1993 to 68 percents in 1998.

Organizational and implementing procedures of each of the literacy projects, was almost similar. This included:

- Literacy centers which were organized in school premises, private residential houses (some rented and some provided free), shacks and shade of trees;
- Primary school directors acted as adult literacy co-coordinators in almost all the centers;
- Some of the literacy teachers were primary school teachers and the rest were recruited from the community on a part time basis;
- Literacy teachers were given small monthly honorariums for the six working months;
- The duration of each literacy project was 18 months altogether, 6 months per year for 3 year and literacy classes were organized for 5 days a week and 2 hours a day;
- Literacy teaching and learning was performed using the curriculum developed during the armed struggle for independence;
- Teaching materials such as: exercise- books, pencils and erasers were provided free of charge to learners.

Assessment findings of the projects initiated after independence largely show that, husbands' pressure, domestic chores and childcare were noted as major barriers for women's participation in the projects. Other reasons that seem to have kept many illiterate adults the literacy projects, economic instability, distance of learning centers from homes and negative (unclear) social attitude toward education.

High dropouts and absenteeism, lack of proper communication and transportation, loose co-operation capacity and experience in management and teaching, and lack of relevant instructional materials were some of the main problems and constraints encountered during the implementation of the aforementioned projects.

ADULT LEARNING AND EDUCATION PROGRAMME IN ERITREA (1998-2008)

Education is not only a basic human right but also an essential component of social and economic development. Investment in education is fundamental for stimulating long-term economic growth and also for improving the overall well being and welfare of the society. Within this framework of development, the macro-policy of the government clearly prioritize education and training as a productive investment in human capital formation with the aim of producing a population equipped with the necessary skills, knowledge and culture for a self-reliant economy. Though there has been a substantial increase in the amount of government expenditure on education in Eritrea in the last 10-17 years, the share of education as a percentage of total government spending is still low.

Moreover, the public expenditure on adult education is very small compared to other components of the education system. But it has increased greatly in the past ten years.

There are also different adult education activities provided by different private organization and Local NGOs. However, their expenditure presented in the above table only covers the activities, which were under the direct control of the Ministry of Education. The data does not also include cost of all adult learning activities within the Ministry due to the lack of adequate data. In the literacy activities undertaken since 1998, the GOE made financial contribution besides the implementation and management of the programme. As agreed with SIDA (Sweden), the financial share of the Government was 1/3 of the total budget required (1999-2002). After 2002, however, the GOE is the sole source of fund of the adult literacy programme. The DAEM in collaboration with other concerned parties within the MOE has been responsible

Table 2. Expenditure on Adult Learning (in Nakfa- local currency)

	Description	Year	Amount	Source of Fund
1	Adult Literacy	1998/9-2001/02	42,450,215.00	The GOE and SIDA (Sweden)
		2002/03-2007/08	65,000,000.00	The GOE and UNICEF
	Total		**107,450,215.00**	
2	Educational Radio Programme			ODA (UK), UNFPA, UNICEF,WB, HAB, Rotary Club, Canada Fund, British Library, American Embassy (Eritrea), Eritrean Diaspora in Washington
		1997-99	1,622,600	
			3,042,100.00	
		2003-04-2005/06	8,250,000	WB, GOE; UNESCO, UNICEF
	Total		12,914,700.00	
3	Basic Vocational Skills Training	1997-2000	6,200,000	GOE, UNDP, NUEW, British Council (Eritrea), OBS
		2001-2002/3	15,000,000	GOE
	Total		21,200,000	
4	Continuing Education	1998-2002/3	2,685,000	GOE
		2003/04-2005/06	3,250,000	GOE
			3,250,000	
			5,935,000	
	G/Total		298,249,830.00	

Exchange rate 1 USD =15 Nakfa

Source: Financial Report of the Ministry of Education 2009

in the overall budget planning and disbursement of funds to the six zobas.

The main problems and constraints encountered during the implementation of the pilot phase literacy project were:

- Border conflict and its consequences;
- Daley of funds;
- Lack of skilled and experienced staffing especially in teaching and preparing literacy primers in some ethnic languages;
- Shortage of proper communication and transportation;
- Limited capacity and work experience of the local publishing companies; and
- Problems in procurement and distribution of materials.

Any encouraging events were observed and recorded in the annual reports produced by the national Literacy Unit during the implementation of the pilot project. The note 70 percent of the 20,000 adult literacy learners enrolled in 1999 complete the 6 months course despite the war wit Ethiopia. The cooperation and determination manifested by the concerned parties and administrators at different levels was another quality input that can be highly considered.

Data collected and processed as the result of the implementation of the pilot project (e.g. data on learner enrollment, source of facilitators, learning achievements, types of literacy building etc.) can serve as base line data for the preparation of the planning and management of the national literacy programme. These data verify the need for a strategic planning to expand to literacy provision throughout the country.

LIBRARY-BASED ADULT LITERACY PROGRAMMES

During the 1960s, the challenge of adult illiteracy became apparent. This challenge was addressed during the 1970s and 1980s by various, often nationally-organized, literacy campaigns. At the same time libraries began to focus on extending their services to marginalized people, particularly through literacy programmes. In the United States, public libraries were offering literacy services dating back to 1963. A planning manual for the American Library Association examined the public library's role in national literacy activities in the 1980s. The study found that public libraries report the greatest involvement in all three literacy roles – collections, instruction, and support services. Over 25% of libraries provided direct literacy instruction and in many of these libraries the programmes had become a part of their traditional public library services. Nearly 50% of the libraries reported involvement in literacy coalitions (Fitzgibbons, 2000). In Victoria, Australia, adult literacy programmes began with a pilot programme at the Council of Adult Education in 1972. By 1982, 10% of the Victoria public library service co-operated in the provision of adult literacy classes and by 1991, this had risen to 25% with another 10% providing support for adult literacy programmes in other ways.(Campbell, 1991: 5).

For various reasons, libraries are the perfect place to provide adult literacy classes. They have ideally easy access to all the resources needed to run an adult literacy programme, including printed and audio books, magazines for all reading levels, videos and newspapers. Most of them can provide space for students and tutors. They are usually centrally located and accessible by public transport. Libraries are friendly and hospitable places, ideally with service oriented opening hours and approachable staff. Adults with low literacy levels often have bad memories of schools and a negative attitude towards formal education. They can be invited to the library to enjoy non-reading activities, such as lectures, movies or discussion groups to facilitate their first step back into learning.

Apart from teaching literacy, the library has to focus its collection development on the needs of its neo-literate users. This means a strong focus is needed on the acquisition of relevant and interesting reading material for adults with low vocabulary or literacy skills. If this material is for whatever reasons not available, the library can develop its own community newspaper, ask the course participants to write their own biography or publish a collection of student writings. These are valuable educational tools which encourage students to write, give them an audience for their products, enable them to gain confidence in their writing abilities and encourage organizational skills.

The library can also help to overcome the problem of gender differences in reading acquisition by maintaining collections of materials that appeal to males and females. Many language classes at school and many adult literacy classes focus on fiction texts, which tend to be less appealing to boys and young men. By providing interesting reading material in the areas of sports, science, politics or Do-It-Yourself manuals, the library can counteract the problem that a large percentage of males are perceived to be slow or non-readers.

In Eritrea, Village Reading Rooms were established to support and extend library services to neo-literate or illiterate in rural areas. As they were mainly established in primary schools, they are today mostly used by pupils and teachers. Nevertheless, they provide a useful and cost effective means of giving access to educational materials in areas where no traditional library service operates.

A strong focus of the last decade has been on using libraries to break the cycle of family illiteracy. The library is a perfect place to offer family literacy programmes as it provides materials and services to all age groups and reading levels. By using the library with their children, parents are setting a good example and help to establish a motivation for reading and a pattern for lifelong learning. In Slovenia, public libraries were among the first providers of intergenerational lifelong learning processes that included children, youth and adults who came together and learned from each other by exchanging knowledge, experiences and viewpoints (Adams, 2002: 30).

The personnel for literacy classes in libraries will come mainly from two sources: the library staff (existing or additional) and volunteers. In order to provide long-term quality service, training and constant development of tutors is crucial. Several countries and organizations have worked on guidelines, some for establishing literacy programmes in libraries, especially public libraries, others for specific types of programmes, such as family literacy programmes, and some for developing training guidelines for library workers. The most comprehensive set of guidelines to date appears to be the Guidelines for Public Libraries Promoting Literacy, developed by UNESCO in 1993 under contract from the International Federation of Library Associations (IFLA) and under the direction of Barbro Thomas.

PROBLEMS AND CHALLENGES OF LIBRARIES IN AFRICAN NATIONS

The situation of libraries differs enormously worldwide. Some countries and regions, such as the United Kingdom, have well-supported library systems, where a well-established library network extends to every community. In stark contrast are countries such as Kenya with only 36 public libraries, Namibia with 48 and Zambia with 22 public libraries (Rosenberg, 2000:7). These libraries were set up under unfavorable conditions, and, as Rosenberg offers in a bleak description of the life cycle of a typical rural African library, their future is often not secured: "Originating from the initiative of a group from the community or an aid agency, their birth is followed by a year or two of rapid growth and a good deal of local publicity and attention. This is followed by a period of slow decline, accompanied by theft, the departure of the initiators, loss of interest among staff and users – the library still exists but signs of life are barely discernible. Sometimes this period continues indefinitely, but often a final stage is reached when all remaining books are removed, stolen, or damaged beyond repair and the premises and staff are allocated to another activity" (Rosenberg quoted by Mostert, 2001).

This description highlights some of the problems and challenges that too often result in a public perception that libraries are not as attractive as they could and should be. The following is a list of the major problems and challenges in the creation, organization, maintenance and use of libraries. These include lack of funds, lack of professional staff, irrelevant material, and colonial mode of librarianship, lack of appropriate training opportunities, lack of needs analysis, ICT challenges, inappropriate buildings and the lack of co-operation and a national information policy.

USAGE ISSUES

There were problems of usage of CRRs housed in classrooms. Adult learners who used the CRRs were reluctant to sit in the small classroom chairs alongside the pupils, who took to the CRRs with enthusiasm. Second, the primary school children made noise and ran around with the confidence of ownership, something that the adult learners resented. If the CRR was indeed to be a community facility, it would have to have its own building.

To date there are 83 functioning Village Reading Rooms. In most cases, the Village Development

Committees have built these structures with drought relief funds, which are provided to be used for income-generating programmes that would enhance the lives of the villagers in face of drought. It is to the credit of most Village Development Committees that they opt to use the funds in projects like building CRR structures. The building project offers employment to unemployed members of the community, who serve as bricklayers, masons, and so forth. Once the building is finished and in use, the question of ownership is never in doubt.

GUIDELINES FOR OPERATION

At the community level, the CRR project is a joint undertaking between the local communities and the Department of Adult Education of Eritrea. The Department of Adult Education provides the staff, stock, and solar panels for electricity; the local community provides the building where the Village Reading Room is located. Guidelines were drawn up for the CRRs at the beginning of the project. They covered the setting up of the CRR, the role of the various stakeholders, and procedures for day-to-day operation. The section on the training and qualifications of the staff specifies that the Department of Adult Education will provide training for Readers' Assistants.

Their training covers:

(i) The role of libraries in relation to literacy;

(ii) Organization and management of CRR materials;

(iii) The circulation system used in CRRs;

(iv) Rules and regulation for CRRs;

(vii) Operation and recording of the solar power lightning system.

The Guidelines state that in order to become a Readers' Assistant one must have:

(a) Passed standard high school examinations or

(b) Attempted Junior Certificate examinations or

(c) Have experience in literacy work.

(Department of Adult Education, Eritrea, 2001)

CONCLUSION

The very concept of community reading rooms in Eritrea is very fertile one. But the success of CRRs like other cooperative efforts depends on the proper mix of enthusiasm, innovative thinking, and caution. There is no doubt that CRRs will be able to deliver the literacy material and teaching far more effectively and efficiently than individual libraries. The existence of various CRRs in different parts of the Africa has illustrated one principle i.e. a successful CRR has to have clear goals, a structure that matches its goals.

One might ask how different the Community Reading Rooms are from ordinary libraries. There is no simple answer. They are rural; they are small, warm, and could even be described as homey. But perhaps what distinguishes the CRRs from other information centers is the clientele. Their sense of ownership and the pride with which they identify with the often small, usually sparse facility that gives them a ticket to the wonderful world of books is a great distinguishing factor. The main objective of the CRR project had been at its inception, and still is, the promotion of reading among rural villagers. Research into the CRR impact on primary and adult readers could yield interesting results in Eritrea.

REFERENCES

- Adams, Sue; Krolak, Lisa; Kupidura, Eva; Pangerc Pahernik, Zvonka: Libraries and Resource Centers: Celebrating Adult Learners every week of the year.,In: Convergence. Vol. XXV, Nr. 2-3, 2002. pp. 27-38.
- Aimut, T. (2001). Planning and management of the National Literacy Programme in Eritrea. Paris: UNESCO.

- Campbell, Lyn; Goldsworth, Carol: Victorian public libraries and adult literacy: a report of a project. South Melbourne, Vic., Victorian Ministry for the Arts, 1991. vii, 74 p., 4°. Annotated bibl.: pp. 53-74.
- Margaret Baffour-Awuah. (2001). Village reading Rooms: Book Outreach in Botswana. School Libraries Worldwide, Gaborone, Volume 7, Number 2, 2001 , 65-71.
- Ministry of Education. (2011) Annual report of Ministry of Education, Asmara.

19

LIS Education in Madhya Pradesh: A Critical Analysis

Kishor John
Assistant Professor (Lib. & Inf. Sc.), OSD, Additional Director, Higher Education, Indore

Indubala Sharma
Librarian, Indore Institute of Law, Opp. IIM, Indore

ABSTRACT

This paper tries to glimpse on trends, challenges, opportunities and present status of LIS Education in Madhya Pradesh, and this whole paper is divided in four parts. First Part deals critical introduction of LIS Education in India and its development alongwith challenges and trends of LIS Education in India. Second Part covers LIS Education in Madhya Pradesh it also covers a brief prologue of various universities of Madhya Pradesh, where LIS Education being run. The Third Part covers a data analysis of various LIS education courses are being run in various universities in Madhya Pradesh, it also takes a glance on Regular and Distance Mode Education in LIS. This analysis has been carried out on the basis of objectives of the study. The Fourth Part is a concluding parts and it covers the threats, recommendations, opportunities and suggestions for improvement of LIS education in Madhya Pradesh.

INTRODUCTION

Library and information science education in India has playing a significant and vital role in the growth of information society through its planned efforts. The aim for providing LIS education is to develop knowledge skills about emerging trends in LIS field and build excellence in the educational system to meet the knowledge challenges of the 21st century and increase India's competitive advantage in fields of knowledge. The education is non ending process which keeps updated and alive the creativity in human beings. The library schools provide education for Library and information science .The schools where the students or learners get mastery through experience or study. Today's society also called knowledge society and in this knowledge/ information society only theoretical knowledge is not enough .With emerging trends the library professional have been also confronted with lots of challenges such as automation, networking and consortia, development of digital library, content management, e-learning, ICT literacy, information storage and retrieval in digital environment, e-learning etc. With appearance these challenges in LIS profession the education program must be design in this manner which meets to cope with newer information technology. The information seeking and information services pattern are also changed with fasting and emerging trends i.e. e-services / online services .with modernization and globalization of education the managements also wants multi skilled persons for his institute who can carried out multitasking operation at their work places, for these the librarian should have not only knowledge about traditional technologies but also have knowledge about newer technologies and their application in LIS filed .The approach of curriculum development should be based on improving knowledge and technical skills, which can encourage the students learning power and competencies and thus the students became valuable at national and international level.

The national knowledge commission also recommended for LIS education that is the LIS education and training (including in-s the service) should be revised and revamped. The Mission on Libraries must assess as soon as possible the Manpower requirements of the country in the area of LIS management, and take necessary steps to meet the country's requirement through LIS education and training. Necessary encouragement and fillip should be given to research after evaluating the research status in this field. A separate well equipped Institution for Advanced Training and Research in Library and Information Science and Services should be set up.[1] LIS education is a life-long process. After initial formal education, it continues in the form of continuing education and staff development.

Development of LIS Education in India: The credit of starting a formal course of library education in India goes to William Alonson Borden and Asa Don Dickenson who established training programmes at Baroda and the Punjab University in 1911 and 1915, respectively. Gradually other universities and library associations like the Madras Library Association (1929), the Bengal Library Association (1935), Madras University (1931), Andhra University (1935), Banaras Hindu University (1941), Bombay University (1944), Calcutta University (1946), and Delhi University (1947) started the library science programme.[2]

After independence, the library science education has taken manifolds. In that period number of library science schools, new colleges, universities, educational institutions and learned societies got functioned. Dr S.R. Ranganathan started a certificate course at Madras Library Association in 1929, which was taking over by the University of Madras, and in 1937 the course was converted into Postgraduate (PG) Diploma in Library Science. University of Delhi was the first university to establish a full-fledged Department of Library Science just before independence in 1946, and started admitting students to the PG Diploma in 1947. In 1951, the university had changed diploma course in to Master in Library Science (MLISc). The course on 'Computer Applications in Libraries' was introduced for the first time in the MLIS programme in 1972. The MPhil programme started in1978. The first Ph.D. was awarded to D B Krishna Rao in 1957, under the guidance of Dr. Ranganathan. At that time it was the only university in the whole of the British Commonwealth conducting PhD programme in LIS.

Later, between 1956 to1959, six new LIS departments were established at Aligarh Muslim University, M.S. University of Baroda, Nagpur University, Osmania University, Pune University and Vikram University. Since 1960s, the number of LIS departments established have continued to increase.[3]

The first distance education program of Library science in India was initiated by university of Madras in 1981 which is foilowed by Dr, B R. Ambedkar Open University Hyderabad 1982. After that number of Open University, schools of directorate and correspondence course were emerged .initially they started certificate, diploma and Graduate level course but later they extended it to PG level course. Now a day many open universities offer Research level course like MPhil and PhD Course.

Presently in India, Library and Information Science (LIS) education are imparted through more than 118 universities and institutions. A total of 105 universities provide Bachelor of Library and Information Science (BLIS) courses, 78 universities provide the Master of Library and Information Science (MLIS) courses, 21 are offering two-year integrated courses, 16 universities provide MPhil in Library and Information Science, 46 universities provide PhD in Library and Information Science and 2 Universities provide D. Litt. Degree.

Besides this, the National Institute of Science Communication and Information Resources (NISCAIR) which was earlier known as the Indian National Scientific Documentation Centre (INSDOC), New Delhi, and Documentation Research and Training Centre (DRTC), Bangalore, provide Associateship courses in Information Science, which are equivalent to the MLIS degree.[4]

To update the LIS curriculum, UGC appointed the Curriculum Development Committee (CDC) 2001 to restructure the courses in LIS, which prompted the LIS schools to include various aspects of Information and Communication Technology (ICT) in their curricula. So far, most of the departments of LIS in India have broadly adopted the scheme as given by the CDC.[5]

OBJECTIVES

The present study highlights the status of library science education in central India region i.e. Madhya Pradesh. In Madhya Pradesh the LIS education started around 1968-70. Presently not mare one university but around more than 10 universities are providing distance and regular courses in LIS. In above perspective we may conclude following Objective:

1. To Explore the importance, opportunities and threats of LIS education system
2. To know development of LIS education in India as well as in Madhya Pradesh.
3. To know LIS education status in Madhya Pradesh.
4. To know which type of amendment is require in LIS education to become technically multi skilled person.
5. To know how LIS can get choice based subject among the society.

6. To know is the present teaching method is needful in 21st century library profession.
7. To know curricula is offering by different open and regular universities In Madhya Pradesh state.
8. To aware the students with LIS profession and ethics to working in traditional as well as in technical environment

TRENDS IN LIS EDUCATION IN INDIA

From the last decade of 20th century the Common trends have noted in the field of library science education is development of ICT skills by which the LIS learner become feel compatible with digital environment today Library science education does not only includes specific library based subjects like classification, cataloguing, reference service etc., but also include some related areas like computer application, statistics, information science management studies and operation research. Various departments are now offering Parallel courses like Master in Information Management (MIM), P G Diploma in Digital Libraries, courses in Health Sciences Librarianship / agricultural Librarianship/Business Librarianship etc.

Now in a present day researcher are mere not only include bibliometry and citation analysis in research but they are also doing variety of Research including scientometry ,webometry, ICT Application in libraries like use of web 2.0 technology (using Blog ,Wikis, Facebook etc.) and six sigma application in libraries by which they enabled library services in very fast and accurate manner present time researcher want to do experimental research in web enabled environment. Usages of ICT application in Library the Library Professionals are also facing some technical problem. The emerging trends in LIS research can help to library professionals to exploring and solving these types of problem. With changing scenario the librarian also interact with variety of user who only wants pin pointed or exhaustive information. It is became possible through implementation of ICT application in Libraries. Library education should be provide in this way that the student will become feel fully capable to working in Web Based environment .To kept this view in mind there are many universities and colleges are providing LIS education not only through computer laboratories but also with software training .

Library schools are emerging as fully- fledged Departments with full time heads and full time teachers. So we can conclude emerging trends in LIS as follows:

- Librarianship-Library and Information Science-Information and Library Studies-Information Studies.
- Library Professionals to Information Professionals
- Traditional Library to Digital Library
- Library Cooperation to Resource Sharing Networks/ Consortia
- Collection Development to Content Development
- Conventional Education to Web-Based Education
- Information Society-Knowledge Society
- Establishment of Knowledge Commission

CHALLENGES AND OPPORTUNITIES IN LIS EDUCATION

LIS education in India has not become receptive to the new emerging situation. The library schools have failed to develop the required knowledge and skills relating to the use of information technology among students. As a result, the graduates from the LIS departments have little competitive potential in the information market and cause of that they are not gathering full job opportunities in market. In India the LIS course varies from university to university and the mostly students are going fail to perform in a technical or a research library. To perform in technical or research Library student should have competencies towards handling of library operation through ICT skills .It may be due to non-uniformity of curricula in national level or curricula is not updated by accreditation bodies with emerging trends. To train the LIS professional in modern age the learning societies and other accreditation bodies try to organizing workshop, conference, symposium, seminar at regular intervals etc.

There are various challenges has been faced with LIS education which are

(a) Non-existent of accreditation bodies
(b) Emergence of new LIS schools
(c) Insufficient Faculty Strength
(d) Lack of proper library facilities
(e) Curriculum updating
(f) Inadequate physical facilities
(g) Little attention for selection criteria
(h) Lack of Apprenticeship Programme
(l) Dual Responsibility[6]

STATUS OF LIS EDUCTAION IN MADHYA PRADESH

The status of LIS education of Madhya Pradesh are given in the succeeding narrations and tables, through these tables It was tried to cover all characteristic:-

1. Awadhesh Pratap Singh University, Rewa

The Awadhesh Pratap Singh (APS) University was established on July 20, 1968 and it got UGC recognition in February 1972. The University is providing holistic quality education to students. Its provide LIS education through regular as well as Distance mode. The LIS course is running under the" Faculty of Arts". The University offer BLIS, MLIS course in Library science education on regular basis as well as correspondence.7

2. Barkatullah University, Bhopal

The University formerly known as Bhopal University was established in 1970 in the capital city of Madhya Pradesh. In 1988, it was rechristened as the Barkatullah Vishwavidyalaya; The University provides LIS education only through distance mode under the umbrella of "Institute of Open and Distance Education". The Institute was established in 1974-75 with the permission of UGC. The university is accredited with UGC & NAAC .The library science education comes under the "faculty of arts". It's providing BLIS and MLIS courses.[8]

3. Devi Ahilya Vishvidhyalaya, Indore

The University Library was established in the year 1964 along with the establishment of the university. The university Library started the Bachelor of Library and Information Science Program from the year 1993-94, as a part of time course, with its goals to train the manpower to manage the libraries of the 21st century. The departments of clib teaching also known as "school of library and information science" which comes Under the "Faculty of Engineering Sciences ".The following regular courses have been introduced during 2006: BLISC and MLIS. .M.Phil in Library and Information Science has started from the academic year 2009-10.the department conduct entrance exam for very limited seat i.e. 30 for BLIS, 30 for MLIS and 20 for MPhil .[9]

4. Doctor Harisingh Gour University Sager:

Doctor Harisingh Gour University Sager is accredited by NAAC and it was **established on 18th July 1946.**The "Department of Library and Information Science", was Establishment On 1970. It provides Library Scienc education. Department has conducted seven Refresher Courses for teachers in LIS and College Librarians with the support and Cooperation of the Academic Staff College of the University. The department is providing PhD, MLIS, BLIS courses. The BLIS and MLIS programs running by university on regular basis as well as correspondence.[10]

5. Jiwaji University, Gwalior

Jiwaji University was established as a teaching and affiliating University on 23rd May 1964, under the provision of M. P. Government Ordinance no. 15 of 1963. The Jiwaji University Gwalior is providing LIS education through Regular mode as well as Distance Mode. The Distance education is helpful for them who can't attend the class due to family obligation or any other reasons. It's also helpful to achieving professional knowledge and to develop awareness in his field at their remote places. The "Institute of Distance Education" in Jiwaji University was established at 1995 to run various professional and conventional academic programmes through the mode of distance education. Under the umbrella of Institute of Distance Education various courses are running the department also known as "school of studies in distance education". Presently the Jiwaji University is providing graduate and post graduate degree course in Library Science through distance mode. The NAAC committee has also, Recognizing to Jiwaji University as best efforts taken by the Distance Education.[11]

In Jiwaji university the department "School of Studies in Library and Information Science" is providing LIS education through regular mode which comes under the "faculty of arts" . School of Studies in Library and Information Science was established in the University in 1984. Its provide quality education and skills to the students according to current needs of the job market. The BLIS, MLIS and PhD. are running by this department. .The Department is extensively engaged in teaching, research and career guidance too. The university select candidate for limited seat like for BLIS the 20 seats for open, the 15 seats for payment and the 5 seats are reserved for NRI same for MLIS.[12]

6. Madhya Pradesh Bhoj Open University

The Madhya Pradesh Bhoj (Open) University (MPBOU) was established under an Act of State Assembly in 1991.the LIS course comes under the category of "Need Based programmes" the university providing BLIS and MLIS program through distance mode.[13]

7. Mahatma Gandhi Rastriya Chitrakoot Vishwavidhyalaya, Satna

Mahatma Gandhi Chitrakoot Gramoday University (MGCGV) was established on February 12, 1991. The university aims is to provide higher education to people living in rural areas. The university is an institute of teaching, learning and research. The department of LIS comes under the "Faculty of Education, Fine Arts, Humanities and Social Sciences." The university is providing LIS education through regular and distance mode.[14] The main objectives of the university are to provide education and dissemination of appropriate technology.

8. Makhanlal Chaturvedi Rastriya Patrakarita Viswavidhyalya, Bhopal

The Makhanlal Chaturvedi Rastriya Patrakarita Vishwavidhyalya, Bhopal, was set up by act of the Legislative Assembly of Madhya Pradesh. There is a wide network of over 500 study centers associated to MCRPV in different parts of the country, where various courses are conducted. It offers BLIS and PhD programme through regular mode. The objective of the course is to provide knowledge of technical working of libraries and to develop skills for information management, i.e., classification and cataloguing.[15]

9. Rani Durgavati Vishwavidhyalaya, Jabalpur

The Rani Durgavati vishwavidhyalaya was established at Jabalpur in 1959. The Discipline of Library and Information Science was introduced in one of the affiliated colleges of the University known as K.P. Guru Bhasha Bharti way back in 1970s. However, the Teaching of this discipline due to one reason or the other could not be introduced at the UTD level. The R.D. University, Jabalpur instituted M.LIB I. Sc. course at UTD level from the year 1998. From the year 2002 the university has decided to introduce BLISc along with the existing MLISc. Course which means that there shall be an integrated two years course leading to BLISc and MLISc. The department known as department of Library and Information science .These courses in Library and Information Science are being run under "Self Financing Scheme(SFS)". The admission is subject to Entrance Test as well as Merit. The future development of this department is to start research work as well as taking University Grants Commission, New Delhi and Department of Science and Technology's projects on automation and networking. Ph.D. in the discipline could be start earlier.[16]

10. Vikram Vishwavidhyalaya, Ujjain

The university was established on the Year 1956 (UGC approved). The library science department of university formally known as" School of Studies in Library and Information Sciences", its comes under the Faculty of "Information Technology." This School offers PhD, MPhil. Post graduate, under graduate courses on regular basis in the field of Library and Information Sciences. The university selects 40 students for BLIS and 35 for MLIS on their limited seat.[17]

Table 1. LIS Education inMadhya Pradesh

No.	Universities	Year of Est.	Courses Run By				
			BLIS	MLIS	MPhil	PhD	Integrated course
1	APSU, Rewa	1968	Y	Y	N	N	N
2	BU, Bhopal	1970	Y	Y	N	N	N
3	DAVV, Indore	1964	Y	Y	Y	N	N
4	DHSGU, Sagar	1946	Y	Y	N	Y	N
5	JU ,Gwalior	1964,	Y	Y	N	Y	N
6	MCRPU, Bhopal	1990	Y	N	N	Y	N
7	MGRCGV, Chitrakoot	1991	Y	Y	N	N	N
8	MPBOU, Bhopal	1991	Y	Y	N	Y	N
9	RDU, Jabalpur	1970	Y	Y	N	N	Y
10	VU, Ujjain	1956-59	Y	Y	Y	Y	N

This table show that total 10 Universities of Madhya Pradesh are offering regular and distance mode of LISc education, the LISc education in Madhya Pradesh was initiated by the Vikram University Ujjain and Devi Ahilya University, Indore has initiated LISc education during the year 1993-94,which is last in Madhya Pradesh. All Universities are offering various degrees such as BLISc, MLISc, MPhil, PhD, and Two Year integrated LISc Course (BLISc and MLISc).

The table 2 shows about when the regular and distance courses of LISc was initiated in various universities of Madhya Pradesh and also reveals that there is a continuous development in number of courses and the types of courses in various Universities in Madhya Pradesh,

Table 2. Establishment of Regular/ Distance LISc Courses in M.P.

S. No	University	LIS Courses						
		BLIS		MLIS		MPhil	PhD	Integrated MLIS
1	A P S U ,Rewa	1968{R}		1968{R}		--	--	--
2	B. U ,Bhopal	1974-75{R}		1974-75{D}		---	----	--
3	DAVV, Indore	1993-94 Part Time And from 2006 {R}		2006 {R}		2010{R}	--	--
4	DHSGU, Sagar	1970{R}	Not Found{D}	1970{R}	Not Found {D}	--	Not found {R}	--
5	J U ,Gwalior	1984{R}	1995{D}	1984{R}	1995{D}	--	1984{R}	--
6	MGRCGV	1991{R}	Not Found {D)	1991{R}	Not Found {D}	--	--	--
7	MCRPU, Bhopal	1991{R}		--		--	1991{R}	--
8	MPBOU, Bhopal	1991{D}		1991{D}		--	Not Found	--
9	RDU, Jabalpur	1970{R}		1998{R}		--	--	2002
10	VU, Ujjain	1956-1959		Not Found		Not Found	Not Found	--

Table 3. Universities Offering LISc Education through Regular Mode

S. No.	Universities	BLIS	MLIS	MPhil	PhD	Integrated MLIS
1	APSU, Rewa	Yes	Yes	No	No	No
2	BU ,Bhopal	Yes	Yes	No	No	No
3	DAVV,Indore	Yes	Yes	Yes	No	No
4	DHSGU,Sagar	Yes	Yes	No	Yes	No
5	JU ,Gwalior	Yes	Yes	No	Yes	No
6	MCRPU,Bhopal	Yes	No	No	yes	No
7	MGRCGV,Chitrakoot	Yes	yes	No	No	No
8	MPBOU,Bhopal	No	No	No	No	No
9	RDU, Jabalpur	Yes	Yes	No	No	Yes
10	VU, Ujjain	Yes	Yes	Yes	Yes	No

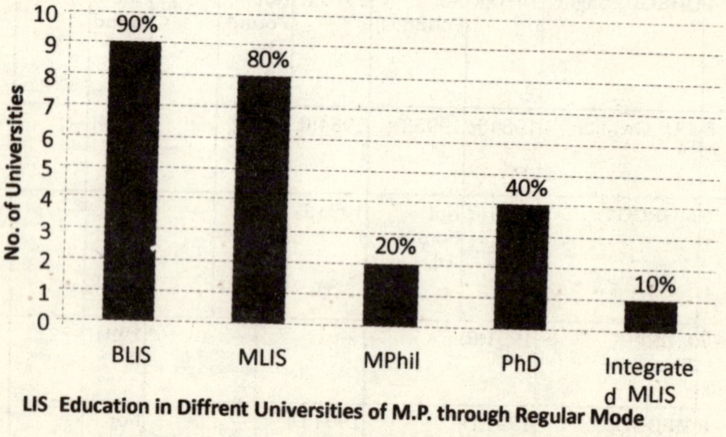

Fig.F 1.F UniversitiesF OfferingF LISc EducationF throughF RegularF Mode

The above table and graph shows that 9 Universities in Madhya Pradesh are offering BLISc Course (i.e. 90%), and 8 Universities are offering MLISc course (i.e. 80%), only two univrsities are offering MPhil (i.e. 20%), four universities are offering PhD Dgreee in LISc (i.e. 40%)and only one university is offering Intergrated Course in LISc (i.e. 10%)through regular mode.

Table 4. Universities Offering LISc Education through Distance Mode

S. No.	Universities	BLIS	MLIS	MPhil	PhD	Integrated MLIS
1	APSU, Rewa	Yes	Yes	No	No	No
2	BU ,Bhopal	Yes	Yes	No	No	No
3	DAVV,Indore	No	No	No	No	No
4	DHSGU,Sagar	yes	yes	No	No	No
5	JU ,Gwalior	Yes	Yes	No	No	No
6	MCRPU,Bhopal	No	No	No	No	No
7	MGRCGV, Chitrakoot	Yes	Yes	No	Yes	No
8	MPBOU,Bhopal	Yes	Yes	No	No	No
9	RDU, Jabalpur	No	No	No	No	No
10	VU, Ujjain	No	No	No	No	No

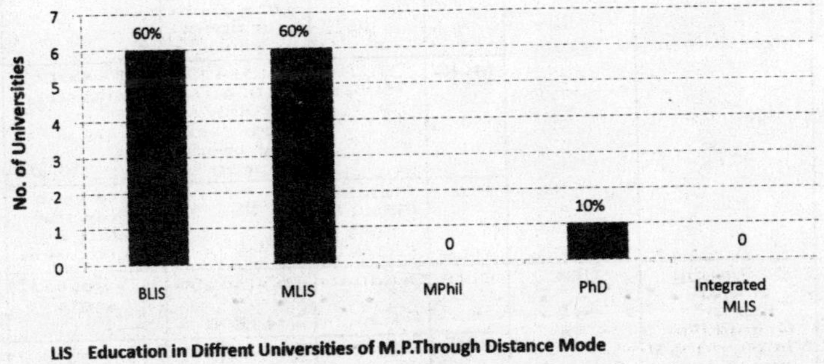

Fig.F 2.F UniversitiesF OfferingF LIScF EducationFhthroug DistanceF Mode

The data shows or implicate that only six unverities are offering BLISc and MLISc Courses through distance mode and only one Univerrrsity is offering PhD Degree through distance mode.

The table 5 shows that most of the Universities are offering BLISc Degree to the graduates and the criteria differ from University to Univerity regarding passing marks at graduate level but the lowest percetange reuired for BLISc is 45% and the highest is 50%, criteria for

Table 5. Status of Universities Offering LISc Education through Regular Mode

No.	University	Accreditation Body	Course	Eligibility	Fees structure	Duration
1	Awadhesh Pratap Singh Vishvavidhyalaya, Rewa	UGC/NAAC-C++	BLIS	Graduate (45%)	----	1 year (2 sem.)
			MLIS	BLIS (45%)	-----	1 year (2 sem.)
2	Devi Ahilya Vishvavidhyalaya	UGC/NAAC-****	BLIS	Graduate (2nd division)	13590 +9900 =23490	1 year (2 sem.)
			MLIS	BLIS	6000+6000 =12000	1 year (2 sem.)
			MPhil.	MLIS (55%)	14590+ 10900 + 11590=37080	18 months (3 sem)
3	Dr.Harisingh Goud Vishvavidhyalya	UGC/NAAC-A	BLIS	Graduates (50%)	----	1 year
			MLIS	BLIS	-----	1 year
4	Jiwaji Vishvavidhyalya, Gwalior	UGC/NAAC-****	BLIS	Graduate (50%)	6115+4225 =10340/- (7000/- extra /sem for open seat)	1 year(2 semester)
			MLIS	BLIS (50%)	6115+4225 =10340/- (7000/- extra /sem for open seat)	1 year(2 semester)
			PhD	MLIS (55%) & 50% (SC/ST)		2-4 year from the date of registration
5	Mahatma Gandhi Rastriya Gramodyog Vishvavidhyalaya, Satna	UGC	BLIS	Graduate	7650+6650 = 14300	. 1 year (2 sem.)
			MLIS	BLIS	8650+7650 =16300	1 year(2 sem)
6	Makhanlal Chaturvedi Rastriya Patrakarita Vishvavidhyalya	UGC	BLIS	Graduate		1year (2 sem.)
			PhD	MLIS		
7	Rani Durgavati Vishvavidhyalaya, Jabalpur	UGC/NAAC –B++	BLIS	Graduate		1 year
			MLIS	BLIS		1year
			Integrated MLIS			2year
8	Vikram University	UGC/NAAC-****	BLIS	Graduation	9270/-	1 Year(2sem.)
			MLIS	LIS G (with50%)	15230/-	1 Year(2sem.)
			MPhil.	MLIS with 55 %		1 Year(2sem.)
			PhD.			

offering admission in MLISc course is BLISc, criteria for offering admission in PhD Degree is MLISc with higher second division. But at present after passing Regulation, 2009 for PhD by the University Grants Commission. All Universities are following the criteria laid down by the UGC for PhD Degree.

Table 6. Status of Universities of Offering LISc Education through Distance Mode

No.	University	Accreditation Body	Course	Eligibility	Mode of selection	Fees structure	Duration
1	Awadhesh Pratap Singh Vishvavidhyalaya, Rewa	UGC/NAAC-C++	BLIS	Graduate in any stream (45%)	Merit	6000/-	1 year (2 sem.)
			MLIS	BLIS (45%)	Merit	....	1 year (2 sem.)
2	Barkatullah University, Bhopal	UGC/NAAC-B	BLIS	Graduate	Merit	6000/-	1 year
			MLIS	BLIS or PGD INLIS	Merit	6000/-	1 Year
3	Dr.Harisingh Goud university	UGC/NAAC-A	BLIS	Graduate	Merit	...	1 year
			MLIS	BLIS	Merit	.....	1 year
4	Jiwaji University, Gwalior	UGC/NAAC-****	BLIS	Graduate in any stream	Merit	10,000	1 year (2 sem.)
			MLIS	BLIS	Merit	10,000	1 year (2 sem.)
5	Madhya Pradesh Bhoj open university	UGC	BLIS	Graduate	Merit	8280/-	1 year (2 sem.)
			MLIS	BLIS	Merit	11040/	1year(2sem.)
6	Mahatma Gandhi Rastriya Gramodyog University	UGC	BLIS	Graduate	Merit	8400/-	1 year (2 sem.)
			MLIS	BLIS	Merit	12000/-	1 year (2 sem.)

The above table shows that there is a no difference in offering distance education LISc in comparison to regular mode as far as the eligibility of admission criterian.

Table 7. List of affiliated colleges from M.P. State universities providing LIS Education

No	Colleges	Affiliated By	Status of College	Estb. Year	Courses BLIB	MLIB	CLISc
1	T.R.S. college of Excellence, Rewa	APSU, Rewa	Govt.	....	Yes	Yes	No
2	AEC Training College And Centre Dept. of Library And Information Science, Bhopal	B.U., Bhopal	Govt.	————	yes	No	Yes
3	Govt. Sarojini Naidu Girls College, Bhopal	B.U., Bhopal	Govt. (Auto.)	1970	yes	No	No
4	Career College, BHEL, Bhopal	B.U., Bhopal	Pvt.	1969	Yes	Yes	No
5	Indira Priya Darshani College, Bhopal	B.U., Bhopal	Pvt.	1995	Yes	Yes	No
6	Chitransh A.D. College, Bhopal	B.U., Bhopal	Pvt.	1995	Yes	Yes	No
7	Rajeev Gandhi College, Bhopal	B.U., Bhopal	Pvt.	1994	Yes	Yes	No
8	Extol Inst. of Management, Bhopal	B.U., Bhopal	Pvt.	1997	Yes	Yes	No
9	Jai Hind Defence College, Bhopal	B.U., Bhopal	Pvt.	1998	yes	yes	No
10	Jawaharlal Nehru College, Bhopal	B.U., Bhopal	Pvt.	1999	yes	yes	No
11	Sardar Ait Singh Memorial Girls College, Bhopal	B.U., Bhopal	Pvt.	1999	yes	Yes	No
12	Gandhi PR College, Bhopal	B.U., Bhopal	Pvt.	1999	Yes	No	No

No	Colleges	Affiliated By	Status of College	Estb. Year	Courses BLIB	MLIB	CLISc
13	Vikramaditya College, Zone-II, M.P. Nagar, Bhopal	B.U., Bhopal	Pvt.	2000	Yes	Yes	No
14	Hemchand Mangilal Sharma College, Bhopal	B.U., Bhopal	Pvt.	2000	yes	no	No
15	Bhoj College, Bhopal	B.U., Bhopal	Pvt.	2000	Yes	Yes	No
16	Chanakya College, Bhopal	B.U., Bhopal	Pvt.	2001	yes	yes	No
17	S.P.B. Memorial College Bhopal.	B.U., Bhopal	Pvt.	...	yes	yes	No
18	Renu College, Mandideep Raisen	B.U., Bhopal	Pvt.	1997	yes	yes	No
19	National College, Vidisha	B.U., Bhopal		2001	yes	no	No
20	Govt, Maharani Laxmibai girls P.G.college, Indore	DAVV, Indore	Govt.	...	Yes	No	No
21	Rediant institute of management and science, Indore	DAVV, Indore	Pvt.	2009-10	Yes	No	No
22	Shri Jain Shwetambar Professional Academy, Indore	DAVV, Indore	Pvt.	2007-08	Yes	No	No
23	Medicaps institute of technology and management	DAVV, Indore	Pvt.	2009-10	yes	No	No
24	IPS Academy, indore	DAVV, indore	Pvt.	...	Yes	No	No
25	M.B. khalsa college, indore	DAVV, Indore	Pvt.	...	Yes	No	No

No	Colleges	Affiliated By	Status of College	Estb. Year	Courses BLIB	MLIB	CLISc
26	Kimti College, Gangiwara Chhindwara	DHSGU sagar	Pvt.	2007-08	yes	no	No
27	Cimti College Ridhora Chhindwara	DHSGU sagar	Pvt.	2007-08	yes	no	No
28	Noble College Sagar	DHSGU sagar	Pvt.	2001	yes	no	No
29	Govt MLB arts and commerce college, Gwalior	J U Gwalior	Govt.	...	Yes	Yes	No
30	Govt girls College, Murar, Gwalior	JU, Gwalior	Govt.	...	Yes	No	No
31	Jain College, Bhind, Gwalior	JU, Gwalior	Pvt.	...	Yes	No	No
32	Oxford College, Gwalior	J.U, Gwalior	Pvt.	...	Yes	Yes	No
33	Rishi Galav College, Morena, Gwalior	J.U, Gwalior	Pvt.	...	Yes	No	No
34	Hikarini Prashikshan Mahila Mahavidhyalaya, Jabalpur	RDU, Jabalpur	Pvt.	———	Yes	yes	No
35	katani Arts and commerce college	RDU, Jabalpur	Pvt.		yes	no	No
36	Kanta Prasad Guru Bhasha – Bharti, Department of LIS, Jabalpur	MRCPV, Bhopal	Govt.	1968	Yes	No.	No

The above lists expressed that there are 36 colleges apart from the University Teaching Departments are offering LISc courses in Madhya Pradesh, if we count the total institutions are offering LISc courses in MP it will up to round about 50.

TEACHING, LEARNING AND EVALUATION METHOD IN REGULAR / DISTANCE EDUCATION

The Distance education is an alternate way of continues education. Most of the universities conduct 10-15 days personal contact programme / classes with student, in that period the student take training and make interaction they also can take help of subject expert of SOS (school of studies) for solving the course related problem. The classes include lectures Guidelines, Theories, Practices, Project, Field Works. The institute personally provides study material / books during the contact classes. Many universities use same kind of study material such as printed/cyclostyled, response sheets, personal contact programme and other assignments. For internal evaluation all universities include assignments projects, pop etc. field work or placement work at given time. But present time most of universities providing distance education through satellite, online lecture, projector etc.

The Regular mode education focuses on teaching, research and career guidance. With Observing the challenges in job market in the new millennium the teaching methods also going to modernize. The Modern teaching techniques such as Lectures, seminars, tutorials, field trips etc are also adopted. For teaching and learning the universities are organize video conferencing, internet facilities and the standard study materials. The technology based study materials play role of teachers. The universities also organized study tour for students as compulsory part of degree .The marks of internal assessment will be made by the teachers. For better learning and teaching several programmes such as conference, refresher course, workshop, seminar etc. also organized by university which is helpful for improving skills among LIS Professionals.

CURRICULUM

There are all universities are running similar pattern for BLIS ,MLIS Level such as on BLIS level the syllabus cover library and society ,reference sources and services ,knowledge organization and processing in classification (theory and practice),Knowledge organizing and processing cataloguing (theory and practice),information technology ,internship programme and for MLIS level the paper included Universal of Knowledge ,classification theory and practice , Advance cataloguing: theory and practice, information technology and implication in library , ,Documentation and Information Science ,Advance Library Organization & Management ,Research methodology, Dissertation and viva-voce etc. The distance mode programme also carries above syllabus. Out of all above 10 universities only two universities are conducting MPhil programme through regular mode, the course is almost same in both universities like information management, Library automation and networking, Research Methodology, Information Technology, Seminar, assignments, dissertation and via-va.

Status of LIS Education and Suggestion: In Madhya Pradesh the most of universities offer distance and regular mode courses for BLIS and MLIS but it is not enough because the library science education still now in a poor condition. At present most universities are not applying modern teaching method and modern Curricula according to need of 21st century market demand. The number of universities only conduct BLIS and MLIS but MPhil and PhD program are not prefer by most of universities because the universities have not adequate and permanent faculty for teaching that's why the MPhil and PhD program runs by universities in least no. The reason behind of these may be varying from university to university or region. When we discuss about distance education the no. of universities conduct only BLIS and MLIS level course. So in this condition what step should be taken by accelerating body for promoting LIS education?

1. To establish uniformity with need of current job market the curriculum should be revaluated and reexamine the accrediting body should have recommended modern curricula.
2. At the national level one accelerating body should be developed for providing finance, scholarship and examining of curricula.
3. The MPhil and PhD should be started in each university for better promotion of research in Library Science.
4. The Fees structure should be kept same at all regular courses and distance course separately.
5. The no. of seats should be increases at the MPhil level.
6. The permanent, qualified and adequate faculty should recruit in all universities.
7. According to changing diversity/responsibilities of library professional the teaching method should also be changed.

CONCLUSION

After observe library science education at all the universities we may conclude that the LIS Education in Madhya Pradesh is not in very good condition .the teaching method, curricula are not fully satisfied to current need. But all of these some universities are providing regular and distance education by the application of new information technology. In teaching method the video conferencing, e-lecture, online lecture, projector, e-learning program also be implemented.

For promoting LIS Education and for updating to

Library professional the there are many programmes are conducting by universities at state /national or international level which becomes very useful for all library professional and teacher's. But the initiative is not enough for promoting LIS Research. The library science education enables to the students at degree and PG level to organize the material, cataloguing, classification, record keeping, shelving, content management ,information storage and retrieval technique in digital environment, creation of online databases, knowledge of software, digital library development, and the MPhil level education enables to students to for library related Planning and working in fully digital environment by which the pin pointed smart services provide to the user within minimum time using SDI and CAS services/ online services .together this education the library science education have many opportunities in various sector like in public/ government/academic libraries, library science teaching, News agencies and organization, foreign embassies, information centre, documentation centre, companies having large amount of databases ,photo film libraries ,museums and galleries etc. .The kind of job may be vary with objective of post and qualification of candidate like professor, Reader, Assistant professor, lecturer, Librarian/Deputy Librarian/Assistant Librarian, senior information source analysts, library and information assistant ,professional assistant, library trainee, librarian community library, documentation officer etc. so with this opportunities the students get beneficial. But all of these the LIS has not choice based subject among the students the cause may be vary from students to students and from their regional places. The modern generation doesn't want to go for such type of job which have less earning the other reason could be the most of the universities not directly offer integrated / Graduate course for LIS like B.E., BALLB, MBBS and other professional courses or minimum seat availability for the courses the no. of people have not sufficient knowledge about Library science education, so for better development and promotion of LIS education some initiatives like online marketing through blogs face book etc. should be started. The open universities having only affiliation for BLIS and MLIS i.e.(100%) but the MPhil and PhD programme not conducted by any university.(0%) this also could be a reason that LIS are not taking new heights in research like other subjects. the same condition carry out by regular courses all above ten universities there all universities conducting BLIS and MLIS course i.e.(100% and 85.7% respectively) but PhD programme followed by only four universities i.e.(50%) and MPhil by only two Universities i.e.(25%) so after many recommendation and many learning programs the LIS education is still now in growing stage except of some universities.

The reality of LIS education is in M.P. is in poor condition. It require amendment with curriculum, time to time refresher courses for LIS professional , financial support for research and other acclivities, recruitment of adequate and qualified faculty etc. selection procedure for teacher and students should be made tough which enables qualified and talented teacher and students also.

REFERENCES

1. www.knowledgecommission.gov.in/downloads/.../wg_lib.pdf
2. publications.drdo.gov.in/ojs/index.php/djlit/article/download/.../43
3. myjurnal.um.edu.my/filebank/published_article/1932/262.pdf
4. eprints.rclis.org/bitstream/10760/10175/1/D7505896.pdf
5. publications.drdo.gov.in/ojs/index.php/djlit/article/download/.../285
6. *http://www.ifla.org/annualconference/ifla75/index.htm*
7. *http://apsurewa.ac.in/Ordinance.aspx*
8. *http://www.bubhopal.nic.in/iode.htm*

9. *http://www.clib.dauniv.ac.in/*
10. http://www.dhsgsu.ac.in/departwebpages.php?depart=56
11. *http://www.jiwaji.edu/distance-education.asp*
12. *http://www.jiwaji.edu/schbool-of-studies.asp*
13. *http://www.bhojvirtualuniversity.com/ada/faq.html*
14. *http://www.ruraluniversity-chitrakoot.org/mgcgv_files/Distance.htm*
15. *http://www.mcu.ac.in/Departments.aspx*
16. http://www.rdunijbpin.org/Libsc.asp
17. http://www.htcampus.com/institute/school-studies-library-and-information-sciences-vikram-university/
18. *http://targetstudy.com/courses/mphil-library-information-science.html*
19. http://www.educationobserver.com/resources/universsities/madhyapradesh.htm

20
Impact of Information Technology on Legal Information Resource And System: A Study With Special Reference to Indian Judiciary

R.G. Yadav
Librarian, D.P. Vipra College Bilaspu
Nidhi Gupt
Asst. Prof. Dr. C.V. Raman Unversity Kargi Road Kota Bilapspur

INTRODUCTION

Apart from computers and information technology, there are emerging areas where judicial work interfaces with different facets of science and technology which constantly change life on earth. Issues for which there are no precedents and are not susceptible to conventional styles of adjudication are being brought before courts and tribunals for resolution. Intellectual Property disputes, environmental disputes and disputes arising from bio-technology are illustrative of this emerging scenario. It will be suicidal to let future judges assume positions of power without even elementary knowledge on technology and technology-related laws which are increasingly becoming common place in society. Environmental litigation is already very much part of judicial.

Work and mere knowledge of environmental laws does not help in dispute settlement. Of course, no lawyer or judge can become an expert on these branches of knowledge; what is expected of them is an informed understanding of the impact of science on life and, wherever possible, an ability to become critical consumers of scientific knowledge without which dispensation of justice in certain disputes will be difficult and dangerous.

The law of evidence is likely to undergo radical changes with standardization of new technologies. The judge will be handicapped if he is unable to appreciate the probative value of new standards and concepts of evidence. The entire technology of DNA printing is an accepted method of proof today in contested parentage and similar disputes. Genetics and reproductive technologies are throwing new light on several questions of fact in which ordinary inferences are no more acceptable. It looks as though the 21st century will herald radical changes in our understanding of human behavior through inventions in biological sciences rather than in social sciences. Naturally, law, concerned with human behavior, has to mend fences with biology and bio-technology in more significant ways than hitherto before.

INFORMATION TECHNOLOGY : DEFINITION

Information technology is the product of fusion of information Science and high technology. Information Science comprise set of practices and related disciplinary studies, which is concerned with the collection, organization, storage, retrival, disciplinary and use. Information Technology is the branch of knowledge that deals with industrial arts, applied science, engineering etc.

UNESCO has defined information Technology as "*the scientific, technologies and engineering discipline, and the management techniques used in information handling and processing ,their application ,computer and their interaction with men and machines and associate social .economic and cultural matter*".

According to the Webster's New Encyclopedia, *information technology is the collective term for the various technologies involved in the processing of information.*

Thus information technology includes computer transmission of information. Thus information technology includes computers technology, communication technology, Multimedia technology, optical technology, networking and Barcode devices technology etc.

PRESENT TRENDS OF INFORMATION TECHNOLOGY

After the launching of the national task on IT, initiative were taken by various state government for IT applications which could benefit the majority of the people. Karnataka was the first state to adopt an IT policy in 1997. Maharashtra, Tamailnadu, Kerala and Andhra Pradesh followed it. In May 1998 The central Government adopted the recommendation of National Task Force of information Technology and software development that such state government should formulate an IT policy. Now most of state government has setup IT department and budget allocation are being set a part of IT promotion .Instate task forces have been set up and action plan have been prepaid. The major weakness for most of policy document is the total folk of rural focus. Kerala and MP claim to have taken sufficient care of this aspect where the local body computerization and network got priority. Kerala's policy clearly declares its commitment to implement local body computerization programmer and to use IT for empowerment of the people and for fulfilling the right to information of the community at large. The policy also has distance focus and developing resource based information system for the state, which could evolve as the knowledge base for the decentralized planning programmer and other developmental initiative in the state. This in turn could be the centre around which an integral decision support tool for planning and management could emerge.

Various Division /Group and associated organization of Ministry of information Technology (MTI) have been engages in number of programmer in collaboration witll different Ministries/Departments of Central and State Government with a view to facilitate the setting up and utilization of IT based service in country. [2-6]

OBJECTIVES

- Reduce space requirements for paper records through the use of electronic files and records. Implement information technology solutions to streamline work tasks, increase productive time, and improve the efficiency of judges.
- Incorporate information technology awareness for judges, every possible venue to encourage the full use of information technology capabilities.
- Improve the accessibility and reliability of videoconference equipment and other technologies used in conducting oral matters with judges.

COURTROOM TECHNOLOGIES

Technology is truly revolutionizing trial processes. The use of technology in the courtroom facilitates case management, reduces trial time and litigation costs, and improves fact-finding, jury understanding, and access to court proceedings. Judges indicate that video evidence presentation technologies improve their ability to understand witnesses and testimony and manage proceedings. Courts are using videoconferencing in a variety of proceedings (as well as for other administrative and training purposes). Technology also has been used in high-profile trials to ensure public safety and enhance the proceedings. The judiciary is continuing to equip courtrooms with a base technology infrastructure and portable equipment that can be shared among courtrooms to ensure technology is available at the lowest cost.

ONLINE SYSTEM FOR CLERKSHIP APPLICATION AND REVIEW

The Online System for Clerkship Application and Review (OSCAR) is an Internet-based law clerk recruitment and application program. Judges can post notices of available clerkships on OSCAR and specify whether they wish to receive applications electronically or on paper. OSCAR streamlines the law clerk application process, enabling judges and chambers staff to receive, sort, and screen applications electronically, to print selected application materials, and to communicate with applicants via email. In addition to submitting their applications electronically, clerkship applicants can also submit electronic requests for recommendation letters to their recommenders, who are then invited to access OSCAR directly and create and upload their letters of recommendation. In 2007, OSCAR completed its third successful year with 800 judges, representing every circuit, using the system, processing a total of over 180,000 applications.

IT TRAINING FOR JUDGES

Since 1992, more than 2,600 judges have been trained in various judges' office automation classes. The curriculum was realigned in fiscal year 2006 to focus more specifically on judges' tasks and functions and correlate the application of information technology to them. Examples of such functions include case management, writing opinions, and trial practices. Judges and court staff are more directly involved in the development of curricula, as faculty in the delivery of programs, and as mentors to assist in local training activities.

There are two distinct components to judges' training: awareness and training. IT awareness activities show judges what applications are available and stimulate interest in pursuing training. National training, workshops, and conferences allow judges to raise the level of IT awareness among their peers and share ideas on how to accomplish judicial tasks using technology. IT training activities provide judges with the skills to master a a particular application, procedure, or task.

THE COHESION OF LAW, JUSTICE, AND TECHNOLOGY

The first duty of a court is to do justice. If the "rule of law" has been declared to be a "basic feature" of the Constitution, which cannot be taken away even by exercising the constitutional power of amendment, then "rule of justice" is definitely above it and deserves the status of the basic feature of the constitution. This is so because the *concept of justice is wider and is of greater importance than the rule of law.* This does not mean that one can ignore the concept of rule of law. It must be appreciated that both rule of law and rule of justice must go hand in hand to make the justice system just, fair and reasonable. In today's world we cannot afford to say that "justice must not only be done but it must also be seemed to be done". The concept of justice requires that:

(1) It must firstly be done in a just, fair and reasonable manner,

(2) It must be seemed to be done, and

(3) It must be "felt" to be done.

Thus, unless this third element of "felt to be done" is satisfied, the concept of justice is not complete because this third element is the most important component of justice delivery system. The public at large in India has a great faith in Indian judiciary and this third element is absolutely essential to maintain and preserve that faith and confidence. A court of law cannot render justice unless the ultimate decision is based on the contemporary law as prevailing in the society. *A decision based on an old law which does not satisfy the requirements of the present situation and environment should be avoided.* In such a situation the efforts of the courts should be to give the law a "purposive, updating and an ongoing interpretation". This position makes the interface of justice delivery system with the information technology inevitable and unavoidable. We cannot allow the dead hand of the past to stifle the growth of the living present. Law cannot stand still; it must change with the changing social concepts and values. If the bark that protects the tree fails to grow and expand along with the tree, it will either choke the tree or if it is a living tree, it will shed that bark and grow a new living bark for itself. Similarly, if the law fails to respond to the needs of changing society, then either it will stifle the growth of the society and choke its progress or if the society is vigorous enough, it will cast away the law which stands in the way of its growth. Law must therefore constantly keep on adapting itself to the fast changing society and not lag behind. *[7]*Thus, we cannot afford to take the information technology revolution lightly.

LEGISLATIVE EFFORTS TO BRING TECHNOLOGY REVOLUTION

To meet the challenges posed by the information technology, the Parliament has enacted the Information

Technology Act, 2000. The aim of the Act is to provide a sound base for e-governance and e-commerce. It must be noted that the e-governance base can be effectively utilized for maintaining a sound justice delivery system. The following provisions of the Act reflect India's determination to utilize the benefits of e-governance for judicial purposes:

1. Legal Recognition of E-Records

Section 4 provides that where any law requires that information or any other matter shall be in writing or type written or in printed form. Such requirement shall be deemed to have been satisfied if such information or matter is rendered or made available in an e-form and accessible so as to be usable for a subsequent reference. The term e-record means data, record or data generated, image or sound stored, received or sent in an e-form or microfilm or computer generated microfiche.*[8]* The term e-form, with reference to information, means any information generated, sent, received or stored in media, magnetic, optical, computer memory, microfilm, computer generated microfiche or similar device. *[9]*Thus as an alternative to paper based record, e-record has been recognized as a medium of communication and storage of information. Further, if an e-record is authenticated by digital signature, it can be produced as evidence for the inspection of the courts. This arrangement is definitely hassle free and more transparent as compared to traditional methods of record keeping. Further, it is not prone to tampering unlike paper-based record, which is difficult to maintain and has its own limitations.

2. Legal Recognition of Digital Signatures

Section 5 of the Act mandates that if any information or any other matter is required by law to be authenticated by affixing the signature, then such requirement shall be deemed to have been satisfied if such information or matter is authenticated by means of digital signature affixed in the prescribed manner. The type of digital signature that shall be used to authenticate an e-record shall be as per the rules that may be framed by the Central Government. The rule may prescribe the manner or procedure to facilitate identification of the person affixing the digital signature. It may also prescribe the safeguards to ensure integrity, authenticity and confidentiality of e-records. Further the rule may provide any other matter which is necessary to give legal effect to digital signatures.[*10*]

3. Use in Government and its Agencies

Section 6 of the Act recognises use of e-records and digital signatures in government and its agencies for filing, issue, grant, receipt or payment of money as an acceptable mode. The Central Government as well as the State Governments is empowered to prescribe the manner and format in which the e-records shall be filed, created, retained or issued. They may prescribe the manner or method of payment of any fee or charges for filing, creation or issue of any e-record.

4. Retention of E-Records

Section 7 is an enabling section, which provides that if any law mandates that documents, records or information are required to be retained for any specific period, then, that requirement shall be deemed to have been satisfied if the same is retained in e-form.

5. Electronic-Gazette

Publication of official gazette in e-form is permitted by Sec.8 of the act. Accordingly, where any law requires publication of rule, regulation, order, bye-law, notification or other matter in the gazette, publication thereof in e-form is permitted. If such publication is made in the e-form, the requirement of publication in the official gazette is deemed to have been fulfilled. When an official gazette is published in printed form as well as electronic gazette, the date of publication shall be the date on which the gazette was first published in any form.

6. Non-Absolute Right

The provisions of Sec.9 mandates that e-governance, as envisaged in the Information Technology Act, does not confer a right upon any person to insist any Ministry or Department of the Central or State Government or any authority or body to accept, issue, create, retain or preserve any document in the form of e-records or to participate in any monetary transaction in the e-form. Thus, sufficient safeguards have been taken to establish a proper and timely e-governance base.

It must be noted that to give effect to these provisions appropriate amendments have been made in the I.P.C, 1860, the Indian Evidence Act, 1872, the Bankers' Books Evidence Act, 1891 and the Reserve Bank of India Act, 1934.These amendments have made these statutes compatible with the "e-justice system".

STATUS OF INFORMATION TECHNOLOGY IN INDIAN COURTS

Ever since NIC took up computerization in Supreme Court in 1990, many applications have been computerized which have impact on masses i.e. litigants. Following are some of the applications which have been successfully implemented at Supreme Court and 18 High Courts and these applications have either direct or indirect impact on the masses.

Supreme Court of India

List of Business Information System(LOBIS)

It is about scheduling of cases to be heard by the courts on the following day. It enabled the Registries of Supreme Court and High Courts in eliminating manual process of Cause List generation thus any manipulation by vested interests. These databases contain details of fresh cases, disposed and pending cases. It is the backbone application of every Court.

Impact

i. As Cause Lists are generated automatically by the computer manual intervention has been eliminated resulting in generation of Cause List in time with out any hassle

ii. Cases are listed strictly in chronological order of date of filing; eliminated irregularities

iii. All cases having the same law point(s) to be decided by the courts are bunched/grouped and posted before one bench. This has helped the courts in faster disposal of cases.

iv. It has become simpler to recall dismissed cases when review petitions are filed.

v. On the spot reliable and instantaneous statistical reports are generated

vi. It has helped Registry of Supreme Court in streamlining its day to day activities to achieve one of the main objectives of COURTIS Project

Filing Counter Computerization

In the Supreme Court of India and all High Courts fresh cases are filed only before the computerized Filing Counters. As the advocates stand in queue for Filing cases before the counters, the data entry Operator enters preliminary details required for Registration such as Party names, advocate details, etc. The computer terminal at the query counter is used to attend to the quarries of the litigants on the spot. The defects, if any, are listed out and handed over to the litigants/advocates for rectification. Time limitation is also checked by the system automatically.

Impact

- The filing process is made easy
- The advocates/litigants need not wait for a long time in the queue
- The amount collected towards Court fee in a day is automatically calculated thus saving the time of court official's time
- Query counter avoids the litigants go around the sections to find out the Filing status
- Filing process is orderly
- Saves time and efforts of advocates and court officials

COURTNIC

This is about providing Supreme Courts' pending case status information to litigants/advocates on any node of NICNET. COURTNIC answers about two hundred queries of litigants/advocates per day all over the country on the status of their pending cases. It is available on nominal charges. Primarily COURTNIC information is available in all NIC-High Court Computer Cells and in some District Court. It has been in use since 1993.

Impact

The response to the COURTNIC from the public is over-whelming, as pending cases information is available at his/her District headquarters. It avoids the litigants to come all over to Delhi from their place. The litigants need not find the status of their pending cases on phone as is the usual practice. Probably this facility is first of its kind in the world.

JUDIS

NIC has brought out Judgement Information System (JUDIS) consisting of complete text of all reported judgement of Supreme Court of India from 1950 to till

Date. (*http://judis.nic.in/*)

Supreme Court's pending Caseson IVR

Interested litigants and advocates can find out the status of their cases pending in Supreme Court on telephone by making use of Interactive Voice. Response System (IVR) free of charge. For accessing this, the phone nos. are: 011-4362062, 4360112.

Cause Lists on Internet (http://causelists.nic.in/)

Causelists are scheduling of cases to be heard by the courts on the following day. The Cause lists of Supreme Court and many other High Courts are available on NIC Web Servers. As the Supreme Court of India and all the 18 High Courts and their 10 Benches are fully computerized, all these courts generate Daily and Weekly Cause lists from the computer servers installed by NIC. The Cause list application is the backbone application of all courts as no court can function with out that day's Cause list. Hence this has become near time critical application in all the Courts.

Immediately after generation of the Cause list most of the courts cyclostyle the stencils cut from the printers attached to the servers for generating thousands of copies running into a few lakes of pages every day. Due to this reason the courts take a lot of time for generation and supply of the Cause lists to the advocates at their offices or residences. Usually the advocates receive the cyclostyled copies of a day's Cause List not before 8 PM. Some High Courts send the Cause lists data on floppy to the Printers for printing thousands of copies. This process costs each High Courts lakes of Rupees every year. By making the Cause lists available on Internet, no High Court is incurring any expenditure as they are using the already available infrastructure and the Software of NIC.

Features

- It is available on Internet
- Cause lists of all High Courts can be accessed at URL i.e. (*http://causelists.nic.in/*)
- Advocates can generate their own Cause list consisting of his/her own cases
- Retrieval through the name of either petitioner or respondent
- Court wise list can be generated
- Judge wise list can be prepared
- Entire Cause list can be printed, if required
- Case no. wise access is possible

Impact

- Advocates are able to receive the Cause lists almost immediately after courts hours
- Advocate can generate their own casuists which will contain only their cases, thus avoiding them to go through hundreds of pages to locate their cases
- As the application is available on Internet, the litigant public can easily find out whether their cases are coming for hearing or not, with out bothering the advocates
- Some courts are considering to reduce the generation of copies of Cause lists, as most of the advocates are dependent on the Internet version of Cause lists, thus the courts can save good amount money on annual basis

NIC has made the Cause lists of the following High Courts on its Web servers apart from the Supreme Court of India

1. Allahabad

2. Andhra Pradesh
3. Bombay
4. Calcutta
5. Chattisgarh
6. Chennai
7. Delhi
8. Gujarat
9. Guwahati
10. Himachal Pradesh
11. Jabalpur
12. Jammu & Kashmir
13. Jharkhand
14. Jodhpur
15. Karnataka
16. Kerala
17. Patna
18. Punjab & Haryana
19. Orissa
20. Uttarancha
21. Sikkim

Ever since NIC has made the Causelists of the Supreme Court of India and High Courts available on Internet, this application has received huge response from the advocates and litigant public. To understand the enormous response the application has received, herewith one week's Day wise Hit statistics are enclosed. On an average *it is receiving 10,000 hits per day.* By any standard, it is a significant number for one application.

For the purpose of illustration, some of the screens associated with the application are also enclosed.

HIGH COURTS COMPUTERIZATIONS

NIC took up computerization of all 18 High Courts and 9 Benches on the lines of Apex Court's Computerizations. NIC implemented the List of Business Information (LOBIS) in all High Court Courts. Some of the High Courts' Cause List are also available on Internet. Many possible applications in all High Courts have been computerized. Most of the High Courts have opened query counters along with Filing Counters for providing pending cases information to the litigants and advocates.

Facilities provided are:

- Cause lists are generated automatically
- Bunching/Grouping is done
- Computer based Filing Counters are opened
- Query counters are available
- JUDIS & COURTNIC are available
- All HCs are connected on NICNET/Internet
- Day to day Judgments and Orders are stored on computers

DISTRICT COURTS COMPUTERIZATION

In 1997, NIC took up the computerization of all 430 District Courts in the country on the lines of High Courts Computerization Project. The basic objectives of the project are:

- to provide transparency of information to the litigants and advocates
- to help the judicial administration in streamlining its activities
- to provide judicial and legal databases to the District Judges

NIC provided three level training programs to the District Court officials. The three levels are:

- **Computer Awareness Programs** for the District

Judges. These training programs were chaired by either the Hon'ble Chief Justice or one of the Hon'ble Judges of the concerned High Court.

- **Supervisory level training** at NIC State Centers. These supervisory level officials were identified and sent to NIC State Centers by the District Courts for training on day to day maintenance of the computers and its peripherals.
- **In-house hands on training** to the District Court officials working on the computer terminals. The District Informatics Officers of NIC posted at the District Magistrates' Office imparted this training.

All officials have been trained on 'District Court Information System' (DCIS) SW. The DCIS Software is a huge general purpose Software package developed for the computerization of District Courts. This software takes care of all aspects of District Courtneeds.

The project is yet to pickup momentum in most of the District Courts for want of interest from the District Court officials. NIC has proposed to conduct another round of Training to the users. *[11]*

CONCLUSION

The advent of information technology has changed the mode of working of almost all the spheres of the life. The justice delivery system has also been benefited by this technological revolution. It must be noted that one of the cardinal rule of interpretation is that the Parliament intends the Courts to apply an ongoing Act a construction that continuously updates its wordings to allow for changes since the Act was initially framed. An enactment of the former days is thus to be read today, in the light of the dynamic processing received over the years. This valuable and golden rule of interpretation has been properly appreciated and adequately applied by the Indian judiciary. Thus, it can be safely concluded that the "E-justice system" has found its existence in India.

REFERENCES

1. http://www.kar.nic.in/fnjpc/report1a.html
2. Indian Journal of Information ,Library & Society vol.20,no.3-4, July Dec.2007 ;p 107-112(Indian journal Technology –Past-Present And Future)
3. Carter, Roger, The information technology : An Introduction 4th es London: pitman.1994
4. Burton, Paul,F: Information Technology and Society. London BLA, 1992
5. Gopinath ,MA Information Technology ,Knowladge processing and Libraries of the future,an interlinked information service. Information Acces through networks Ed by MA Gopinath an E. Ramareddy,Hyderabad, Booklines,1996.
6. Lenk,K. Information Technology and Society. In Friedricks, G. Microelectronics and Society -1982, pp273-310
7. Justice Bhagwati in *National Textile Worker's Union v P.R.Ramakrishnan,(1983) 1 SCC 228, at p. 256.*
8. Sec.2 (1) (t) of IT Act, 2000
9. Sec.2 (1) (r) of IT Act, 2000
10. Sec.10 of IT Act, 2000
11. http://www.it in law.htm Ministry of Information Technology National Informatics Centre Courts Informatics Division.